# PowerPoint 2016: The Basics

This workbook was created and copyrighted in 2014 by Luther I
It has been edited by Tammy Gammon, Ph.D.

Microsoft®, Word®, Excel®, Outlook®, and PowerPoint® are registered trademarks of
Microsoft Corporation. Screenshots used with permission from Microsoft.

Conventions used:

Keyboard:
Keys to be pressed are enclosed in parenthesis such as: press (Enter).

Text to be typed, when included in an exercise step will be shaded. For example:
Type *No Fault Travel* and then press (Enter).

Mouse Operations:

Click:   refers to clicking the left mouse button

Right-click: refers to clicking the right mouse button

Drag: refers to clicking and holding the left mouse button down and moving the
mouse

Published by:

Pro-Aut Training and Consulting, Inc.
1024 Hemlock Ave.
Lewiston, ID  83501

For discounts on quantity orders, check out our website:  www.Pro-aut.com

You may also visit www.LutherMaddy.com to contact the author and see additional
resources available for this workbook.

# Table of Contents

# Lesson #1:  Getting Started

## In this lesson you will learn to:
- *Create a PowerPoint Presentation*
  - *Add Text to Slides*
  - *Create New Slides*
  - *Choose a Design template*
- *Save a Presentation*

## Lesson #1: Getting Started

PowerPoint is a program included in Microsoft Office and allows you to create exciting and informative slideshow presentations. You can even use it to create presentation handouts and even videos to place online. This course will introduce you to the basics of PowerPoint and get you comfortable enough with this program to create your own presentations for meetings, trainings, or wherever you may need a slide presentation.

### Starting PowerPoint

When you start PowerPoint you have the choice of opening a previously created presentation, or creating a new one. You will begin this lesson by creating a new presentation. When you do choose to create a new presentation, you can create a blank presentation or create one based on themes and templates. For this course, you will begin by creating a new, blank presentation.

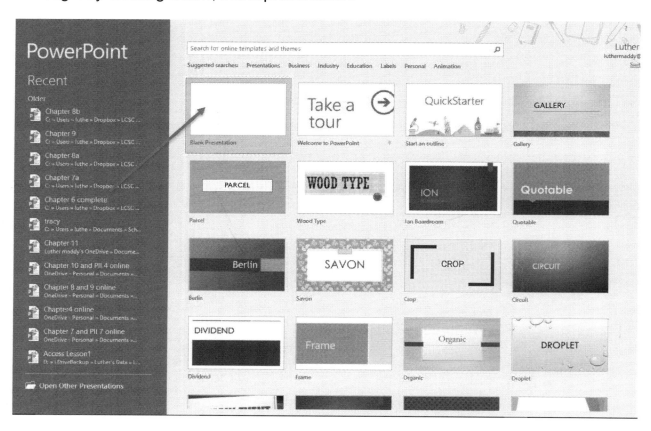

1.    **Start PowerPoint and choose Blank presentation from the available themes.**

When you choose Blank Presentation, PowerPoint begins with a blank slide. You can begin your presentation by adding text to this slide, or as you will soon learn, change the layout of the slide before you begin.

---

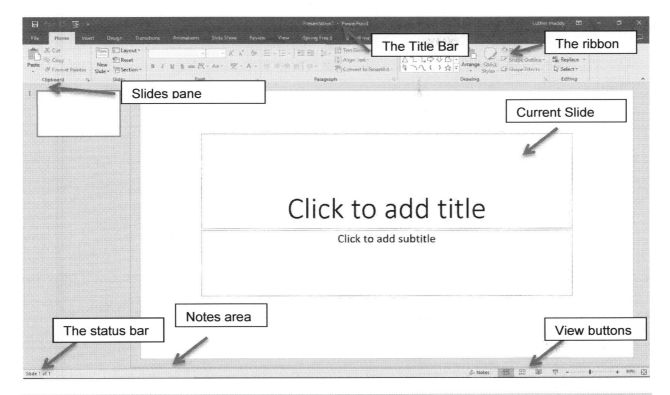

## The PowerPoint 2016 Window (Normal View)

As you start a new, blank presentation PowerPoint will display a title slide and be in Normal view. Before you learn more about those two terms, take a few minutes and explore the screen you now see.

**The Title Bar:** Identifies your window by name, including the program and current presentation name. As with any other program in Windows, you also have control buttons that allow you to Close, Restore, Minimize, and Maximize the window.

**The Ribbon:** The ribbon displays many tabs. The ribbon allows you access to features related to the tab name. The most commonly used features are found on the Home tab.

**Current slide pane:** This area allows you to enter text and other objects into the presentation's slides.

**Slides pane:** The tabs at the top of this pane allow you to switch between viewing icons of the slides or an outline of the text on each slide.

**The Status Bar:** Displays the slide number you are currently working on and the number of total slides in the presentation. It also displays the name of the design template you choose to give your presentation a consistent look.

**View Buttons:** The view buttons are shortcuts to the various views in PowerPoint: Normal, Slide Sorter, and Reading view. (Clicking on the Slide Show shortcut button will begin your presentation at the currently viewed slide).

**Notes pane:** This area allows you to add speaker's notes to slides. Its use will be covered in a later lesson.

## Creating a presentation

When you first open PowerPoint to start a new presentation, PowerPoint defaults to the Normal View. The normal view allows you to view and edit one slide at a time. You will learn to use the other views shortly.

Also, when you begin a new presentation, PowerPoint defaults to the Title Slide layout for the first slide. PowerPoint has several slide layouts to choose from and each of these layouts are pre-formatted with placeholders for text and objects. Many presentations begin with a Title Slide and this is why PowerPoint uses this layout at first. You will now view the slide layouts available in PowerPoint using the Layout tool in the Home tab.

**2.    Select the Home tab if it is not displayed and then click the Layout tool.**

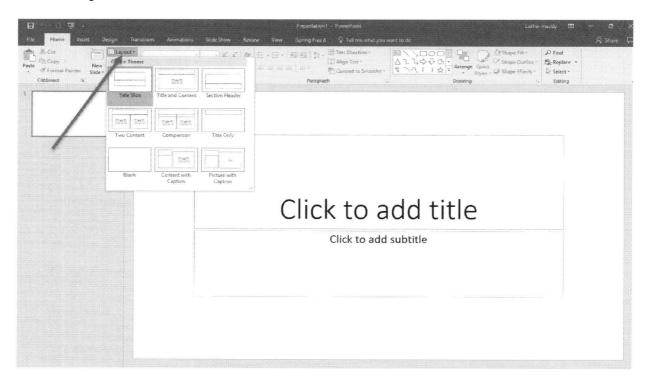

PowerPoint will now display the slide layouts available to you. For now you will stay with the Title slide layout for this first slide.

---

**3.    Click Title Slide layout if necessary to begin creating your presentation.**

You will notice that the title slide layout has two text place holders or text boxes, the title placeholder and the subtitle placeholder.  Each of these placeholders already has attributes selected for you such as font size, color, and centering.  Each PowerPoint slide layout has different attributes already set for you.

Now that you have selected the layout for your presentation's first slide, you are ready to add some text to that slide.

**4.    Click in the title placeholder at the top of this slide and type No Fault Travel Agency.**

You do not need to press (Enter) after typing the text unless you want to move to another line to add more text.

**5.    Click in the subtitle placeholder and type Specializing in Worldwide Travel Adventures.**

Your slide should look like the example. Notice that the subtitle placeholder contains different formatting than the title placeholder.

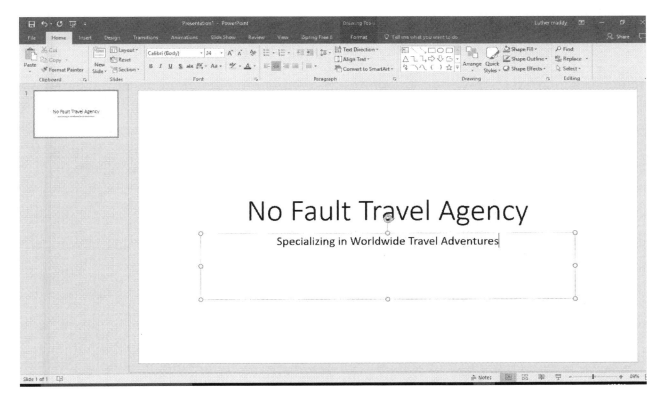

## *Inserting a new slide*

Your slide show starts with one slide. You will usually want to create additional slides for your slide shows. To add additional slides you can use the New Slide tool on the Home tab.

## 1. Click on the New Slide tool in the Slides group on the Home tab.

Clicking below the icon on the words, New Slide will let you see a list of slide layout choices.

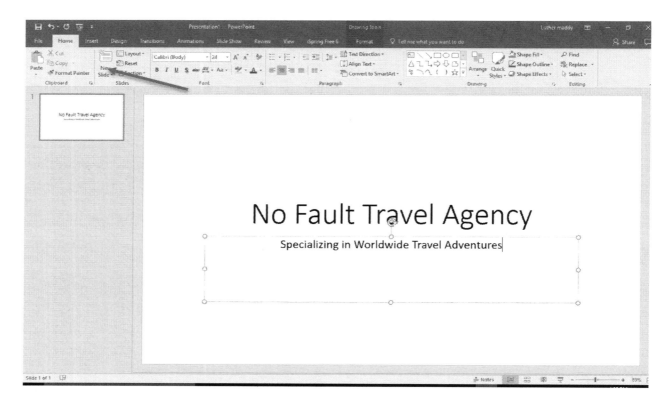

As you click this tool you will see the Slide Layout choices. Here you can choose the layout for this new slide. You will choose a different layout for the next slide in your presentation.

**2. Select the Title Only slide layout as the layout of this new slide.**

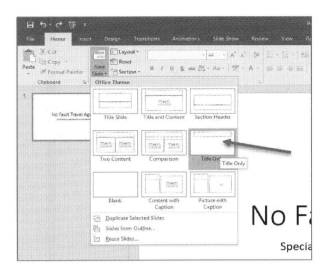

PowerPoint will now add another slide to this presentation. This slide layout has only one placeholder at the top of the slide.

**3. Click in the title placeholder in the new slide and type *We Specialize In...* and then click outside the placeholder.**

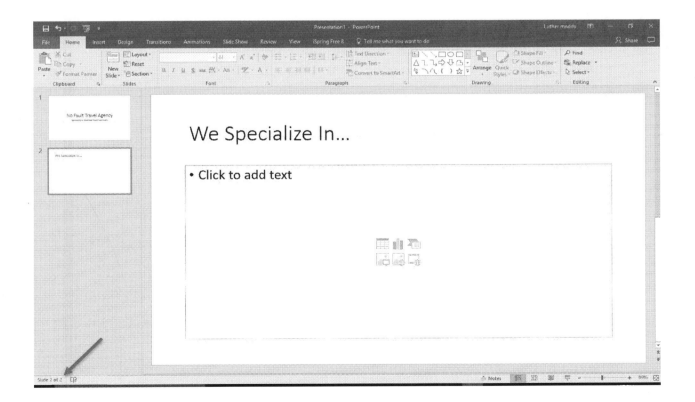

If you carefully examine the status bar you will see that it tells you which slide you are working with and the total number of slides in the presentation.
You will now insert a third slide into this presentation.

**4.    Click the New Slide tool and choose the Title and Content layout.**

If you accidentally click too high on the new slide tool and get a new slide before choosing the correct layout, you can click the Layout tool and select the correct layout.

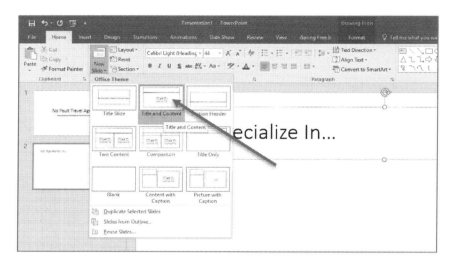

The Title and Content slide layout automatically adds bullets to items in a text list. This layout also allows you to easily add a chart, table, video or other items to the slide.

**5.    Click in the title placeholder of the third slide and type *Vacation Packages*.**

**6.    Click in the bottom placeholder and type *Customized Vacation Packages* for the first bulleted line.**

You should see that PowerPoint automatically added a bullet to this item.

**7.    Press (Enter) to add another bulleted item and then type *Group Rates*.**

**8.    Press (Enter) and type *Guided Tours* for the last bulleted line in this slide.**

Your third slide should look like the example on the next page.

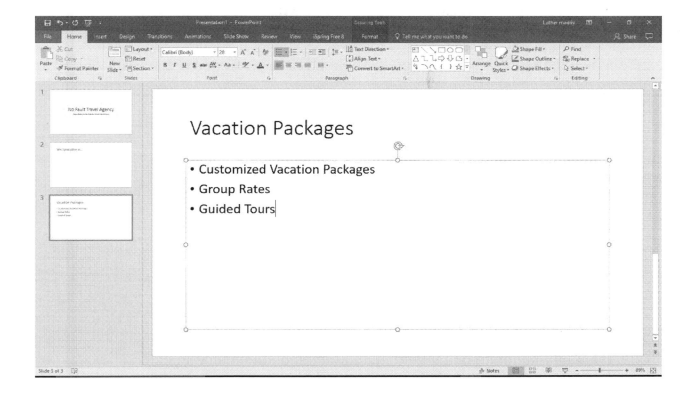

> **Presentation tip:** Keep text to a minimum on presentation slides. Too much text makes the slide difficult to read and confusing. No more than six bulleted items on a slide is a good rule.

You will now add a fourth slide to this presentation.

**9.   Click the New Slide tool again and add another slide with the Title and Content layout.**

When you click the New Slide icon, PowerPoint will insert a new slide with the Title and Content layout. Since this is the layout you want for this slide, you could simply click the icon and save a step.

**10.   In the title placeholder of this new slide type *Cruises and Tours***

**11.   Click in the bottom placeholder box and type the following bulleted text, pressing (Enter) after each line except the last.**

- *Discounted Cruises*
- *All Cruise Lines*
- *Ports of Call Worldwide*

Your fourth slide should look like the example on the next page.

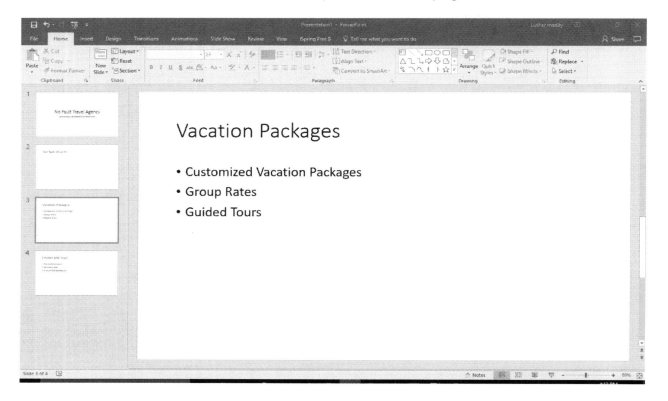

You will now insert a fifth slide in this PowerPoint presentation.

**12.    Insert a new slide with the Title and Content layout.**

**13.    Click in the title placeholder and type** Business Travel

**14.    Type the following bulleted text in the bottom placeholder.**

- *Corporate Rates*
- *E-Tickets*
- *Special Hotel and Rental Car Rates*

Your fifth slide should look like the example on the next page.

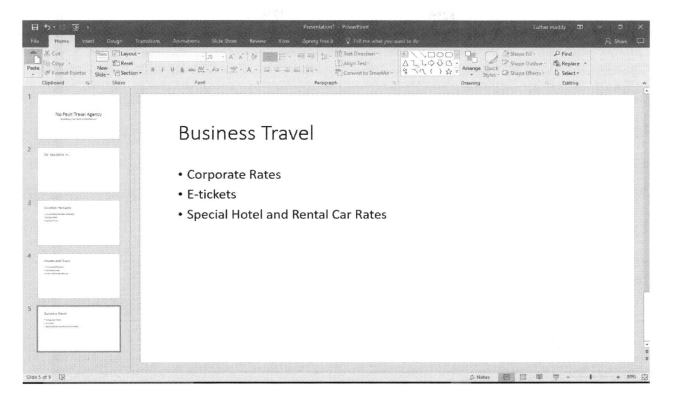

**15.** **Insert a sixth slide using the Title and Content layout. Add the text as shown in the example slide below.**

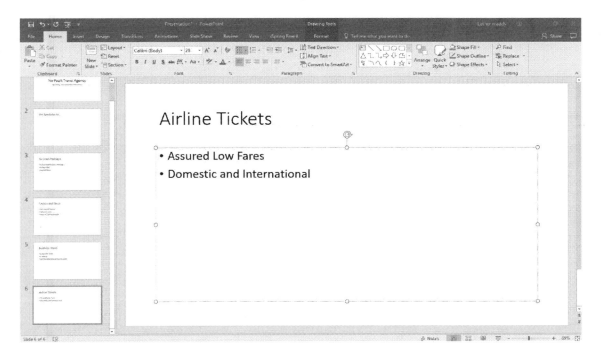

Now that you a basic slide show, it is time to add a design theme to make it more attractive.

Currently your slides have no design background because PowerPoint's default design theme is blank. Fortunately, PowerPoint has several themes available to dress up the appearance of your slide show. PowerPoint's design themes make it easy to give your presentation a consistent and professional look. You can access the Slide Designs from the Design tab on the Ribbon.

**1.     Click the Design tab on the ribbon.**

You should now see the presentation themes along most of the ribbon. There are some other design tools available on this tab as well. You can click the down arrow (more arrow) at the right of the template icons to display even more themes.

**2.     Click the More down arrow in the Themes group on the Design tab.**

**2.     After exploring the available themes, select the Facet theme.**

When you click on a theme, PowerPoint applies that design to the entire presentation. If you do not have this theme on your computer, choose any other theme you like.

> **Presentation tip:** You can change the theme of your presentation at any time simply by choosing another one from the list. PowerPoint will then reformat your entire presentation with the new theme.

Your presentation is now much more attractive. So far, you have learned to add new slides and select slide layouts, but there is much more to come. Since you will be using this presentation for the additional lessons in this course, you will want to save it to ensure you do no lose all this work.

### Saving Presentations

If you do not want to lose the slides you have created, you will need to save the PowerPoint presentation. Saving permanently stores the file on your computer's hard drive, the company server, or even the cloud. Saving it allows you to retrieve (open) it again when you need it later. You should develop the habit of saving frequently. If you do not, you may have to re-create unsaved slides. You can save presentations using the Quick Access toolbar or by accessing the File menu.

**1.   Click the File tab and then choose Save.**

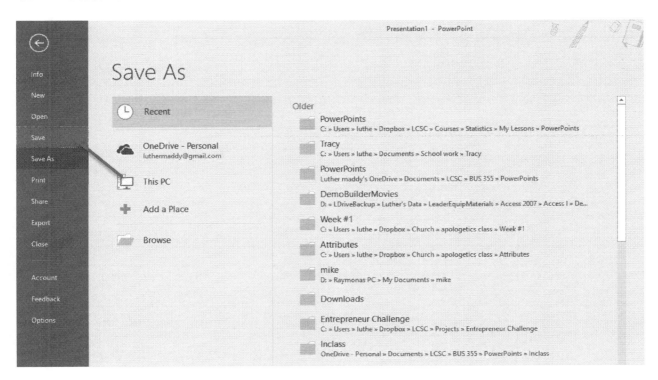

**2.   In the backstage view, click Browse and navigate to the Documents folder.**

This workbook will assume you are storing your files in the Documents folder. Depending on your computer's setup, this folder may be called My Documents. You may choose, or be instructed to choose a different folder. Where you store this file is not all that important. Remembering the folder you choose makes finding your files much easier when you need to use them again.

### The Save or Save As dialog box

When you choose the Save command, PowerPoint will display the Save As dialog box. This is because you have not yet saved this file and PowerPoint needs you to give this file a name to save it. You will use this name to refer to this file when you want to use it again. After naming the file the first time you save, you can then save any additional work very quickly with the Save command and not have to worry about typing the name.

Your Save As dialog box may be a little different than the illustration, depending on your operating system version. In addition to the file name, this dialog box allows you to specify the drive and/or folder you want to store this file in. If you are in class, your instructor should provide the proper saving location for you, but the Documents folder is often a good choice when you are in the learning process.

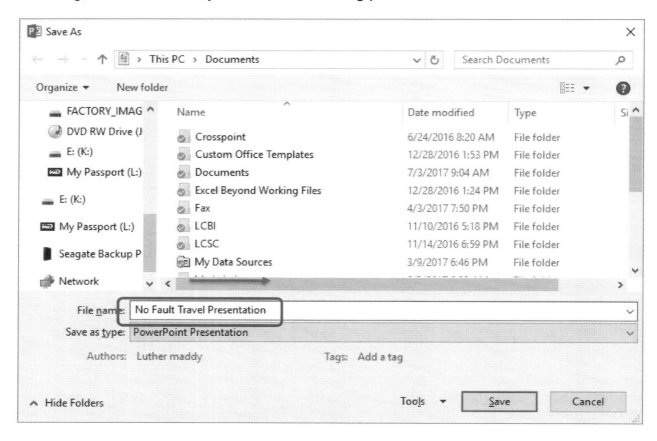

2. In the File name text box, type *No Fault Travel Presentation* and then click Save.

---

You will now close your presentation.

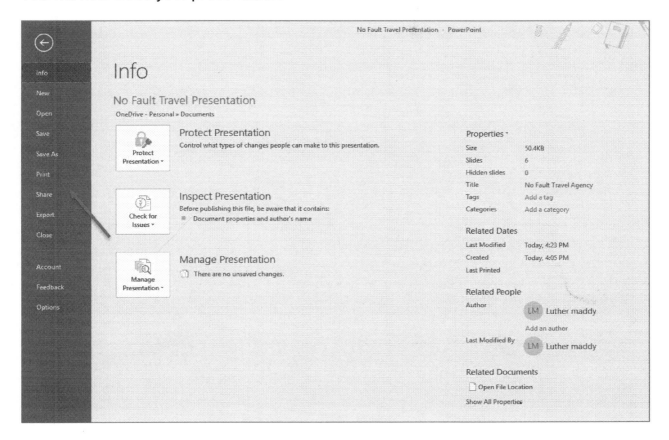

## 4.	Click on the File tab and then click Close.

If you have made changes since the last time you saved this presentation, PowerPoint will ask you if you want to save before closing.  In most cases, you would choose yes, by clicking Save when you see this question.

You have now closed the No Fault Travel Presentation and there is no presentation currently open.  You could now use the File menu to either open an existing presentation or create a new one.  You will do both in upcoming lessons.

# Lesson #2: Exploring PowerPoint View Options

## In this lesson you will learn to:

- *Open an Existing Presentation*
- *Display Slides Using Different Views*
- *Run a Slide Show Manually*

## Lesson #2: Exploring PowerPoint View Options

PowerPoint has several views you can use as you create and edit your presentations. Among those views are Normal, Slide Sorter, and Notes Page. You can access these views from the View tab on the ribbon. You will now see how these views can assist you in creating and editing your slide shows.

### *Opening a saved presentation*

You will explore PowerPoint's views using the No Fault Travel presentation. That presentation is currently closed, so you will need to open it again.

When you click the File tab, PowerPoint will display the most recent presentations you worked on. This provides a very quick way to re-open a file you were just working with, such as the No Fault Travel presentation. Since you will not always see the presentation you want in this list, this lesson will have you use the Open dialog box. Here you can browse different folders to find the file you are looking for.

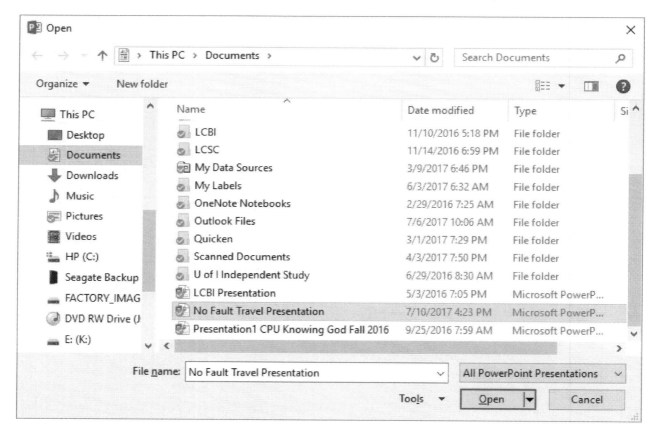

1.   **Click the File tab and choose Open. Then, click Browse and navigate to the Documents folder.**

If you saved this file in a different folder, navigate to that folder.

---

Because PowerPoint remembers the last few files you were working on, clicking Browse was not really necessary in this case. But, this is the steps you can take to find a file that is not listed among your recent files.

## 2.    In the list of files, click on *No Fault Travel Presentation* to select it and then click Open.

You may have also noticed that PowerPoint displayed a list of your most recent presentation files when you first chose the Open command. This is a very quick way to open a file you just worked on, such as the No Fault Travel presentation. However, this lesson showed you how to open a specific folder to find a presentation file in case the one you wanted was not in the most recent list of files.

### Normal View

When you open a presentation, PowerPoint will display it in the view you were using when you saved the presentation. When you saved this presentation, you were in Normal View, so that is the view PowerPoint displayed when you opened the No Fault Travel presentation.

This Normal View allows you to see the slides as they will display in the slide show. The normal view allows you to edit each individual slide. This view also displays thumbnails of all the slides. The Normal View also gives you access to the Notes area below the current slide. This Normal View is the view you will use most often as you are creating and editing slides.

When you open a presentation in Normal View, PowerPoint will display the first slide, which is what you are viewing now. If you wish to view or edit other slides, there are several ways to move to and view the other slides in normal view. Some of those methods will be explained in this lesson.

## 3.    In Normal View, press the (End) key.

PowerPoint will now display the last slide, #6, in the presentation in Normal View.

## 4.    Press the (Page Up) key.

PowerPoint will now display the slide just before the last slide in the presentation, #5, in Normal View.

In PowerPoint, the (Home) key takes you to the first slide and the (End) key, as you just tried, takes you to the last slide.

You can also use the mouse to move from slide to slide.

## 5.     Locate and click the Previous Slide arrow on the right scroll bar.

Clicking this arrow will move up one slide. In this case it moves you to slide #4. There is also a Next Slide arrow that will move down one slide.

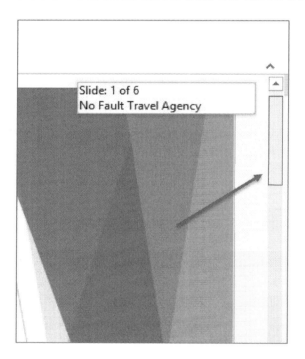

To move from slide to slide, you can also drag the button on the scroll bar. As you drag this button up or down, PowerPoint will display the slide you will land on when you release the mouse button.

## Outline View

You can display the Outline view by clicking the Outline View tool in the View Tab. The Outline View displays the titles and main text on each slide in an outline format. In this view, you can enter and edit text. You can also rearrange the slides in this view. Working in Outline view is one way to organize and develop the main content of your presentation.

**1.    Locate and click the Outline tool in the View tab.**

PowerPoint will now enlarge the Outline pane and display the text of all the slide in outline view at the left edge of the screen.

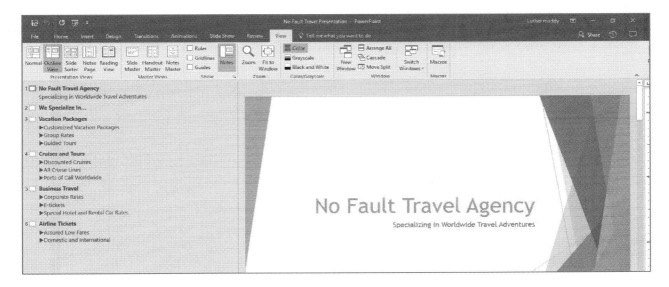

You will now use PowerPoint's Outlining tools to change the indent level of some bulleted text in a slide. PowerPoint calls changing the indent level promoting or demoting. To demote or promote a bulleted line, you must first select the line you want to work with.

**2.    In the Outline pane, right-click the second bulleted line in Slide #4 (*All Cruise Lines*).**

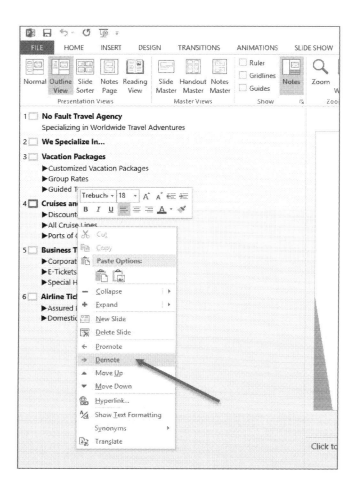

You will now see a shortcut menu. Among the options available on this shortcut menu are PowerPoint's Outlining tools including, move up, move down, promote, and demote.

## 3.    Click the Demote tool in the submenu.

Demoting an item causes it to be indented further into the page. You will also see that change reflected on the slide.

## 4.    Now right-click on the text you just demoted and choose the Promote option in the shortcut menu to undo the demotion you just made.

The bulleted item should return to the same level as the other items on that slide.

## Slide Sorter View

The Slide Sorter View displays all the slides of the presentation as thumbnails. In this view you can copy, move, delete, or add slides. You can also add slide transitions, which you will do in a later lesson.

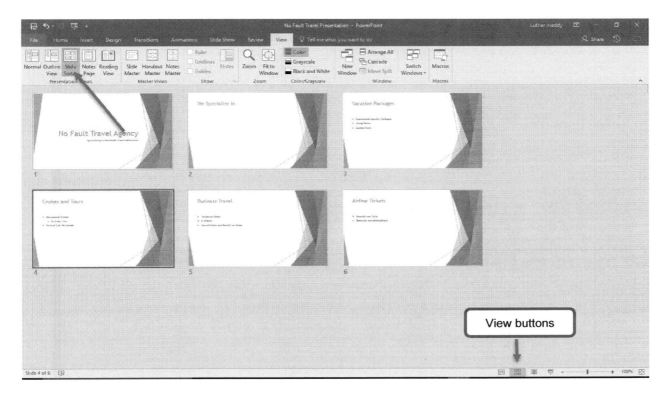

View buttons

**1.     Remaining in the View tab click the Slide Sorter tool.**

You could have also used the View button on the status bar to change the view. Either way is fine. Now that you are in Slide Sorter view, you will rearrange a couple of slides. If you have many slides in your presentation, you can decrease the Zoom setting quickly using the Zoom shortcut at the bottom right of the PowerPoint window.

**2.     In the Slide Sorter view, click the Airline Tickets slide, 6, to select it. Then, drag it between slides 4 and 5.**

You will hold the mouse button down as you click and drag to move. As you drag, you will see the slide move and when you release the mouse the slide will be in its new location

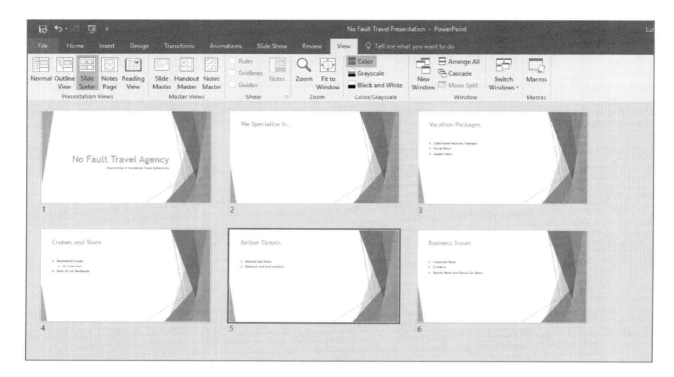

When you release the mouse the Business Travel slide should be slide #6 and the Airline Tickets slide should be slide #5.

You can also move slides in the normal view by dragging the slide thumbnails in the slide pane to the left of the slide you are currently viewing.

### Notes Page View

The Notes Page View is used for typing presenter's notes. Speaker's notes you type in this view will not be displayed in your slide show, they are designed for the presenter to use. You may print the notes separately using Print options, which you will learn in a later lesson.

The notes area is visible and usable while you are in Normal view. To add a note, you can simply click in that area and begin typing. The Notes Page view expands the notes area, making it easier to type larger amounts of text in this area. You can expand the Notes Page area view by choosing Notes Page from the View tab. In the Notes Page view, you will see the slide and an expanded notes area.

**1.    Display the View tab on the ribbon and click the Notes Page tool.**

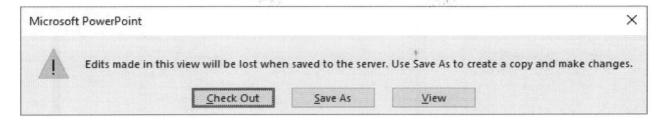

If you saved your presentation in a shared folder such as OneDrive, you may see this message when entering the Notes Page view. If you do, you can choose the Check Out option or choose Save As and save it on a local drive.

You will now type presenter notes for the first slide.

**2.      Ensure you are viewing the first slide. Press the (Home) key to go to the first slide if necessary.**

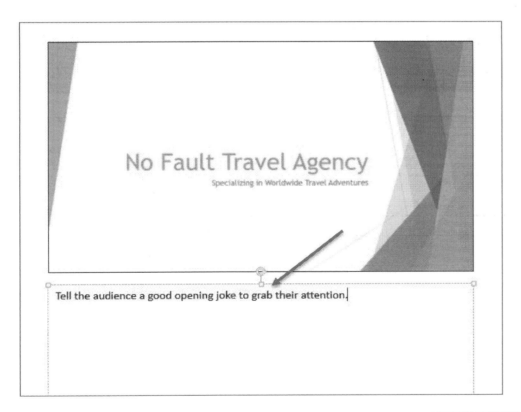

**3.      Click in the Notes placeholder and type *Tell the audience a good opening joke to grab their attention.***

You will now return to Normal view.

**4.  Click the Normal tool on the View tab to return to Normal View and close the Notes Page View.**

### Running the Slide Show

When you run a slide show, PowerPoint will display one slide on the full screen, which might be a projector or large screen if you are presenting to a group or even in a virtual meeting.  The presenter will usually advance the slides manually, when he or she is ready for that particular slide.  It is also possible to set up slide timings and have the slides advance automatically.  This mode is useful when you want a self-running demo for a kiosk, trade show or other event where you do not want to advance the show manually. In this course, you will learn to run slide shows that rely on the presenter to advance the slides.

You can start the slide show from the Slide Show tab.  After selecting this tab you will have the option of starting the slide show from the beginning, slide #1, or from the current slide if you are viewing a slide other than the first one.

You can also start the slide show using the View buttons in the bottom right hand corner of the window.  Running the slide show from the View buttons will start the presentation at the slide you are currently viewing.  Using the Slide Show tab gives you the option of doing either.

### Using Presenter View

When you are presenting before a group you may have two monitors, one for you, the presenter to view, and the other may be projected on a large screen for the audience to view.  With its presenter view feature, PowerPoint 2016 lets you control the slide show as well as view the speaker notes during the presentation.

The screenshot below gives you an example of the presenter.  This view shows the slide currently being shown in full screen view as well as a smaller view of the next slide.  You will also notice the speaker notes you just created displayed for the current slide. This view allows you to advance the show manually as well as end the show.

One very exciting feature with this version is the ability to zoom in on a particular portion of the slide during the show.  You can do this using the Zoom tool, which looks like a magnifying glass below the currently displayed slide.

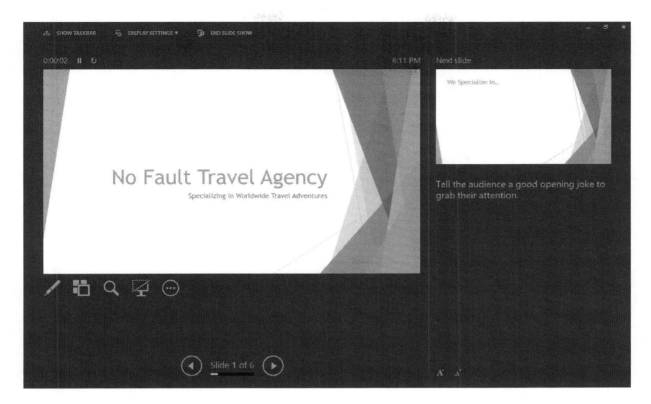

Since you may or may not be using two monitors while you are going through this workbook, this course will assume you are using only one monitor while you are learning this program. When you can use a computer with two monitors, experiment with the Presenter view. You should find it very useful. For now, you will continue this course assuming you are using only one monitor.

**1.     Click the Slide Show tab on the ribbon.**

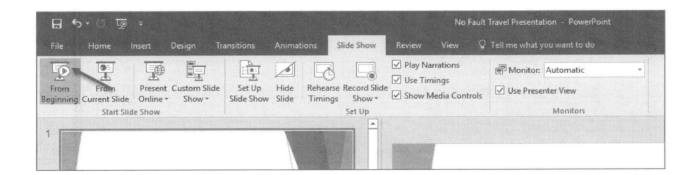

**2.     In the Start Slide Show group, click the From Beginning tool.**

You will now manually advance the slides in this presentation. You can use the mouse to advance by simply clicking the mouse. You can also use the keyboard or mouse to advance from slide to slide.

Using the Keyboard:
The (**Home**) key goes to the first slide.
The (**End**) key goes to the last slide.
The (**Page Down), (Enter**), (**Space bar), (Right Arrow)** and (**Down Arrow**) keys goes to the next slide.
The (**Page Up), (Backspace), (Left Arrow)** and (**Up Arrow**) keys moves to the previous slide.

The (**ESC**) key stops the slide show and returns to the PowerPoint window.

3.    **After viewing the first slide press (Enter) to display the next slide.**

4.    **Press (Enter) to advance to the next slide. Continue pressing (Enter) until the slide show has completed.**

When the slide show completes, PowerPoint displays a blank, black screen. You can press (Enter) when you reach this screen to return to PowerPoint's editing mode.

When you end the slide show, PowerPoint returns you to the view you were in before you started the Slide Show.  In this case, you returned to Normal View because you were in that view when you started the show.

**4.**      **Save and close your presentation.**

8/15

# Lesson #3:  Editing Presentations

**In this lesson you will learn to:**
- *Edit Text*
  - *Enhance Text*
  - *Change Alignment and Indenting Levels*
- *Modify Bullet Style*
- *Add Textboxes*

## Lesson #3: Editing Presentations

You have created a basic presentation, added a design theme and seen it in action. Now, you will learn to edit and enhance text on the slides. This lesson will also cover changing the bullet style displayed on a slide. You will also learn to add textboxes to slides so that you are not dependent on the predefined slide layouts for the appearance of your slides.

### 1.    Open the *No Fault Travel* presentation.

When you open a presentation, PowerPoint will return to the view your presentation was in when you saved it. For this lesson you will work in Normal view, so you will need to change to Normal view if necessary.

### 2.    Display the View tab and choose Normal if you are not in this view.

You should now be viewing the first slide in normal view.

### *Editing Text*

To edit text within a text box just click on the text you want to work with in that placeholder. Then, position the insertion point, cursor, where you want to begin editing. You can then use the backspace and delete keys to delete unwanted text. You can insert additional text by moving where you want the text and typing.

To delete more than one letter at a time you can use (Control+Delete) to delete the word to the right of the insertion point. (Control+Backspace) will delete the word to the left of the insertion point.

### 3.    On slide 1, double-click the word *Worldwide* and type *Global*.

You have now replaced the word Worldwide with Global.

You can easily select one word using the double-click method. Triple clicking will select one paragraph of text.

### *Enhancing Text*

If you have not yet typed the text you want to enhance by changing attributes like font size and color, you can simply turn on the enhancement and type the text. When you no longer want to use that enhancement, turn off the enhancements you turned on.

To enhance text already on a slide, you must select that text before you can enhance it. You can select text within text boxes using several methods such as clicking and dragging, double-clicking to select a word, or triple-clicking to select a paragraph.

In this portion of the lesson you will enhance existing text and also explore different methods of selecting text.

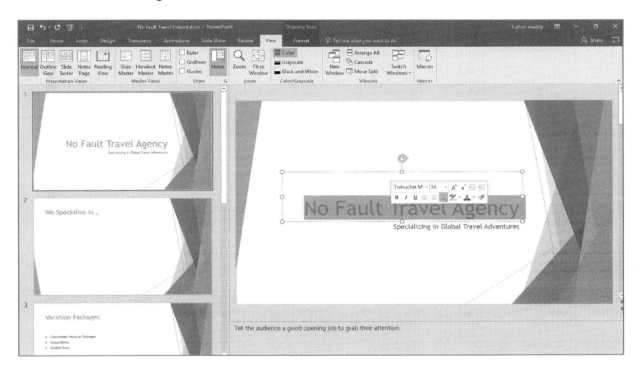

3.     **On slide #1, Triple-click the title *No Fault Travel Agency* to select it.**

Triple clicking selects an entire paragraph, which in this case is only one line. Text that is selected will be highlighted in gray.

4.  **Ensure the Home Tab is displayed and then click the Font drop down list arrow and chose *Comic Sans MS* as the font.**

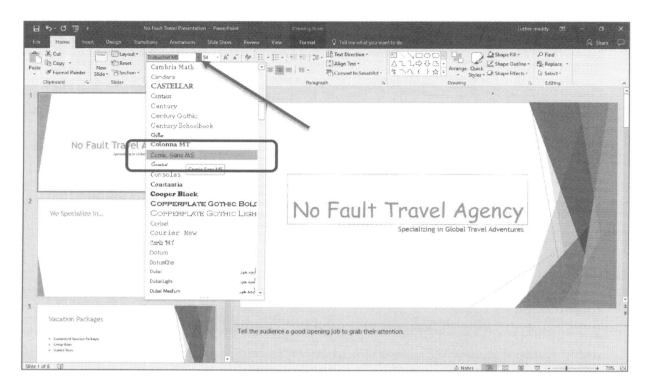

After you click the font name, you should see that PowerPoint changed just the text you had selected. You will now change the font size of this text.

5.  **Ensure the title is still selected then click in the size drop-down list and change the font size to 60 points.**

When you changed the font size to 60 points you should have noticed that the title automatically grew to two lines. This is because the textbox that holds this title is not wide enough to handle the enlarged text. If you determine you want the title to appear on one line only, you can reduce the size of the font until it fits within the box. Or, it may be possible to simply increase the size of the textbox slightly to have the enlarged text fit. This is the approach you will take in this lesson.

6.  **Carefully move the mouse to the sizing handle at the center left side of the title text box.**

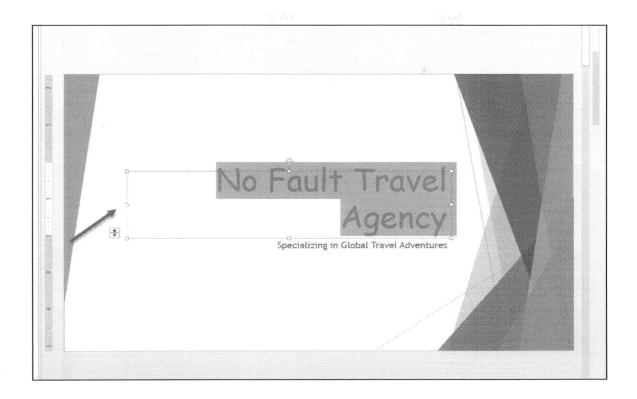

The sizing handle appears as a white square on the edge of the title textbox outline. You will know you are in the correct place when the mouse pointer appears as a double headed horizontal arrow.

**7.     Carefully drag the mouse pointer to the left until you see the text all on one line.**

As you drag the mouse you will see the box re-size.  When the box is large enough, the text will move onto one line.  When you release the mouse, you should notice the enlarged title now fits in the title textbox.

8. **Make sure the title text is still selected then click on the Color drop-down list in the Font group.**

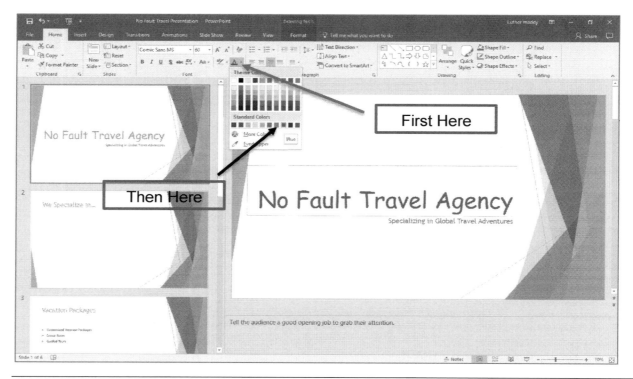

**9.     In the Color submenu, select the blue color.**

You have now changed the font, size, and color of the title.  The color you selected does not correlate very well with the color scheme of this design template, but you will change the design colors later in this course.

**10.     Click on any slide thumbnail in the Slides pane.**

Doing this will de-select the text you were working with.  This causes PowerPoint to leave the text editing mode and allows you to use slide navigation keys like (Home) and (End) to move to additional slides.  If you remained in the text editing mode, the (Home) and (End) keys would move to the beginning and end of the text within that textbox.  You could also have de-selected this text by clicking in a blank area of the slide you were editing.

### Changing Text Alignment

The theme you have applied to this presentation aligns all the text on the slide against the left edge (left aligned).  You may recall that when you first created the slides, the titles were centered.  When you apply a theme you may find that it has changed alignment and even font style, size, and color.

You can easily "override" a theme's default alignment and other settings by simply selecting the text you want to change and applying the change.  You will now change the text alignment on some of your slides.

You have already learned some methods of selecting text in PowerPoint.  In cases where you want to change all the text within a textbox (placeholder), you can select the textbox and then apply the change.  This is the method you will use to change the alignment of the title on the last slide in your presentation.

**1.     Press the (End) key to go to the last slide, Business Travel.**

Because you de-selected the title text, you moved to the last slide.  Now, you want to work with the text within a slide, so you will now select the text you want to work with, which in this case is the title of this slide.

**2.     Click anywhere in the title on this slide to display the outline of its placeholder.**

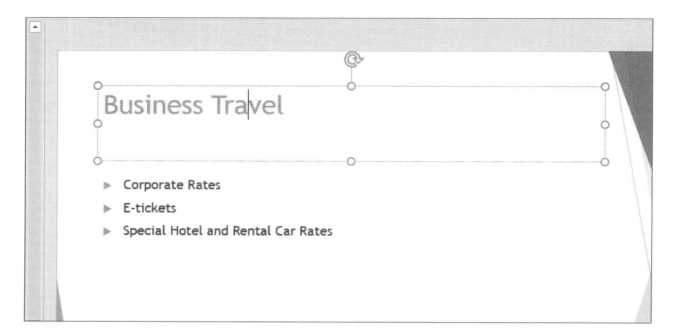

When the placeholder outline displays dashes it indicates you are in the text editing mode. In this mode you would need to select all the text that you want to change within the text box. By selecting the textbox itself, all the text within it will change.

**3.   Carefully click on the outline of the title textbox.**

You should notice the outline of the title placeholder is now solid.

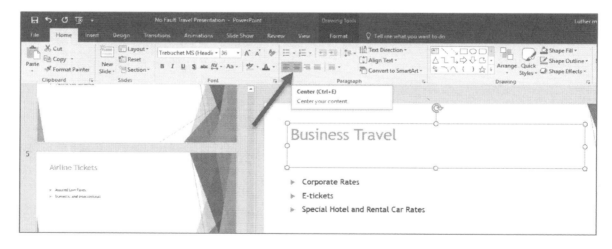

**4.   Now, click the Center tool in the Paragraph group on the Home tab.**

When you point to this tool, PowerPoint will show you the name of the tool and the keyboard shortcut for that command if there is one available. You should now see the title centered on this slide.

As you saw earlier, the theme you apply may change fonts and alignment. The theme also controls how far from the edge of the slide the bulleted items start and how much space there is between the bullet and the start of the text. These settings are called indent levels. In this portion of the lesson you will adjust the position of the bulleted items. To do this you will use the Paragraph dialog box.

## 1. In Normal view, go to slide # 3, Vacation Packages.

You want to change the position of all the items in this bulleted list. Because you want all three lines to change you must select all three lines. If you only selected one bulleted item, only that line would change.

You could select all the bulleted items by clicking and dragging or by selecting the entire placeholder as you did earlier when you clicked the edge to get a solid outline. This lesson will now introduce you to a keyboard shortcut, (Control+A). This keyboard shortcut command selects everything within a placeholder.

## 2. Click once in the placeholder with the bulleted list and press (Control+A).

All three list items should be selected.

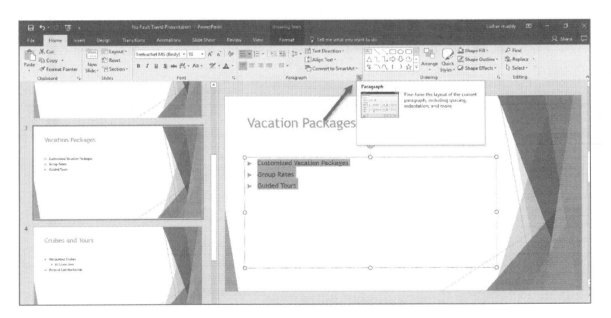

## 3. Click the paragraph dialog box launcher on the Home tab.

You should now see the Paragraph dialog box. Here you can easily change the indent position and line spacing for the selected text.

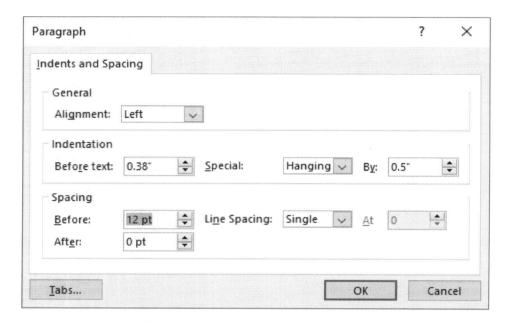

**4.** **In the Indents and Spacing tab, change the Before text setting to 1" and the Hanging to .5". Also, change the Before spacing to 12 points and then click OK.**

The Before text setting controls the position of the text in relation to the left edge of the slide. The Hanging setting controls the spacing between the bullet and the start of the text. The Before spacing setting controls the spacing between the paragraphs.

As you clicked OK and returned to the slide, you should see those changes applied. The bullets should start further in the slide and there should be more space between the bullet and the text.

## *Modifying Bullets*

The theme you applied also determined the bullet style. You may have noticed that the bullets changed after you applied this theme. As with other formatting options determined by the theme, you can also change the bullet shape.

You will now change the bullet shape on Slide #3.

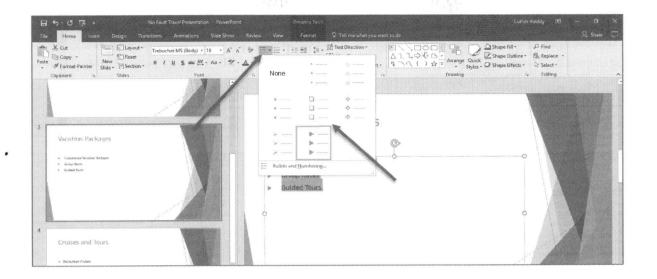

1.   **Ensure the bulleted items on slide #3 are still selected, then click the drop down list arrow associated with the Bullets tool.**

You now see a list of the bullets associated with this theme. For this lesson you will pick a pre-defined bullet. If you wanted to customize the bullet color or pick a different shape, you could select Bullets and Numbering from this menu.

2.   **From the list of available bullets, select the hollow square bullet shape.**

Only the bulleted items on this slide will have the shape you selected. If you wanted to change the bullet style on all existing and new slides, you can change the Master Slide layout and that will be covered in an upcoming lesson.

You should also be aware that when you overwrite some theme formatting options, such as bullet style and font changes, they will remain in effect even when you change themes.

## Adding a text box to a slide

In order to add text to a slide outside the pre-defined placeholders, you must add another text box. By manually inserting textboxes you can place text anywhere you want on a slide. The text box option is found in the Insert Tab.

After creating a textbox, you can then add text to it and move it or re-size it as you wish. In this portion of the lesson you will now add a text box to the first slide of this presentation.

1.  **Click on a slide thumbnail to de-select the bulleted list, then press the (Home) key to go to slide #1.**

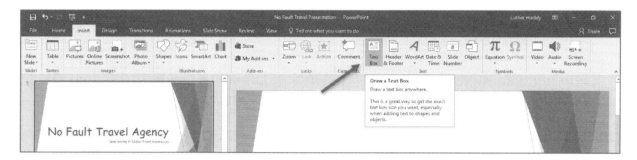

2.  **Display the Insert Tab and then click the Text box tool.**

3.  **Click in a blank area below the subtitle at the bottom of the slide.**

You will notice PowerPoint inserts a small placeholder when you click. This text box will expand as you add text to it.

4.  **Type *Bon Voyage!* in the new text box.**

After creating a textbox you can format the text or reposition the placeholder on the slide. In this portion of the lesson you will move the textbox near the top of the page, change some font attributes, and rotate the text box.

**5.** **Click carefully on the edge of the new textbox and drag it to within a few inches of the top of the slide as shown in the example.**

With the textbox still selected, you should notice a hollow white circle just above it. This is the rotate handle and you can use this to rotate the textbox on the page.

6. **Use the rotate handle to rotate the textbox so it appears as the example. Change the font size to 44 and the font color to light green as shown.**

### Moving a text box to another slide

Placeholders, textboxes, and other items can easily be moved or copied from one slide to another. In this portion of the lesson you will move the textbox you just created to another slide. To move a textbox, you will simply select it and use the Cut and Paste tools on the Home tab.

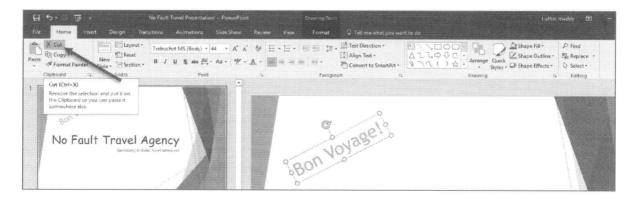

1. **Click on the edge of the new textbox to select it. Then click the Cut tool from the Home tab.**

Remember, the solid lines let you know the entire placeholder is selected. The textbox is now removed from the title slide and you will paste it onto the Cruises and Tours slide.

**2.** **Move to slide #4, Cruises and Tours, and click the Paste tool on the Home tab.**

You will now see the textbox in this slide. You will now move it to an appropriate location on the slide.

**3.** **Drag the textbox down and to the right as shown in the example.**

**4.** **Save and close the presentation.**

# Lesson #4:  Working with Themes and Slide Masters

**In this lesson you will learn to:**
- o *Create and Modify Slide Masters*
- o *Modify Color Schemes*
- o *Create and Use Custom Themes*

## Lesson #4:  Working with Themes and Slide Masters

### *Modifying Slide Masters*

A Slide Master contains the default settings for placeholder locations, font attributes, background colors, and bullet styles.  The configurations of the master slides are determined by the theme applied to the presentation and even the blank presentation theme you start with has master slides.

Modifying a master slide will cause those modifications to appear on all slides that use that master.  Every slide layout such as the Title Slide, Title and Content, and all the others, have its own master slide.  There are also master slides that also control the appearance of Handouts and Notes Pages.

You can access the master slides from the View tab. In this lesson we will modify master slides and then save our changes as a new theme.

## 1.    Open the *No Fault Travel* presentation.

Before modifying the master slide layout, you will add a slide number to all slides in this presentation, except the title slide.

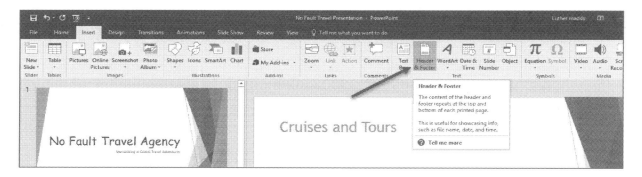

## 2.    Display the Insert tab and click Header and Footer tool.

You will now see the Header and Footer dialog box.  Here you can choose to have the current date and/or slide number appear on all slides, the one slide you were viewing, or all slides but the title slide.  Where the date and slide number appear are controlled by the master slide for the theme you are using.

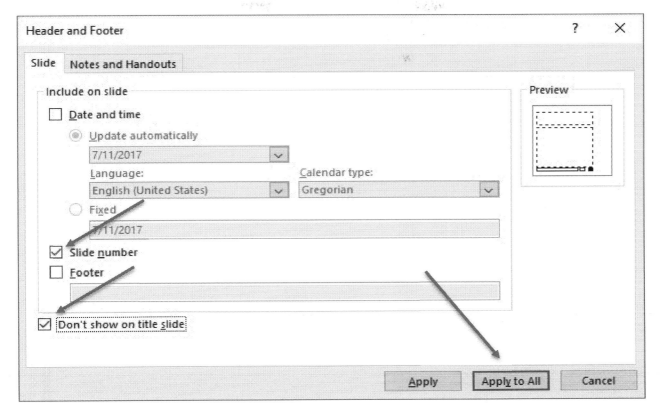

**3.** **In the Header and Footer dialog box, click the Slide number and Don't show on title slide check boxes. Then click Apply to All.**

You want the slide number to appear on all the slides in this presentation, except the title slide.

As you examine any slide but the title slide, you should see the slide number in the near the bottom right of the slide. It may be hard to locate now, but you will change its size and color in this lesson. The position and color of the slide number placeholder are controlled by the master slide layout.

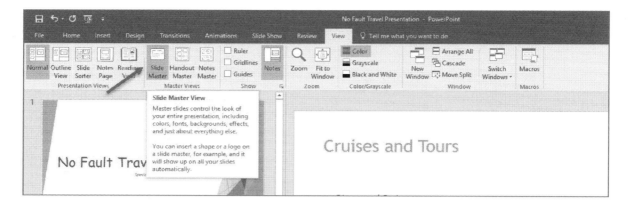

## 4.    Click the View tab and choose Slide Master.

After selecting the Master Slide View, you should see several master slides, one for each available slide layout.  The very first slide at the top of the list controls the some appearance elements of all the slide layouts.  You will now change the master color scheme of this theme.  This change will affect all existing slides and any new ones you may add to the presentation.

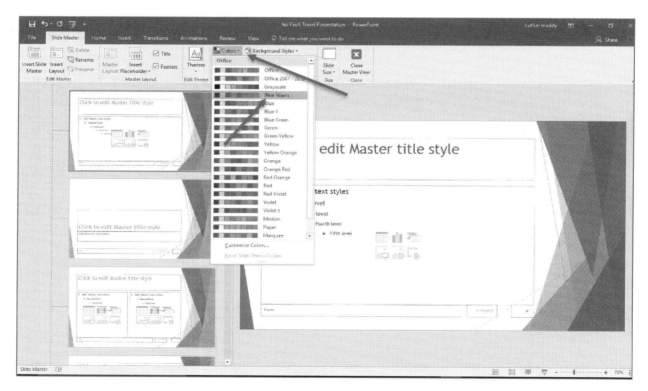

## 5.    In the Master Slide View tab, ensure you are working with the very top Master slide, then click the Colors drop down list arrow and choose Blue Warm.

As you chose this color scheme, all the master slides will reflect that change. So too will the slides you have already created in this presentation.

Now you will change the size of the slide number so it is more clearly visible.

6. **Ensure that you are still viewing the slide at the top of the list of slide layouts in the Master Slide View. Then, select the slide number textbox near the bottom right of the slide.**

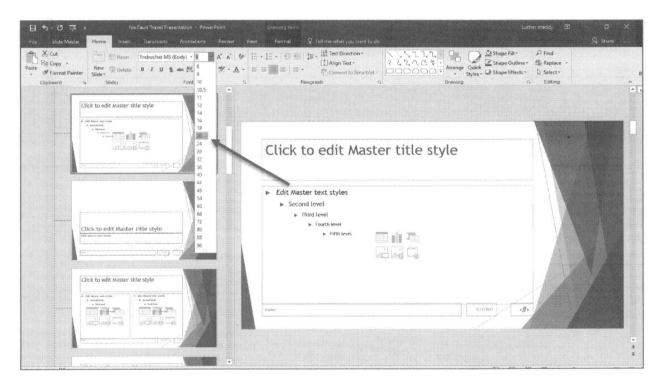

7. **With the slide number textbox still selected, display the Home tab and change the font size to 20 points.**

This change will affect the slides in the presentation, and any new one you add.

Now you will return to the normal view and verify that the changes you made to the master slides appear in your presentation.

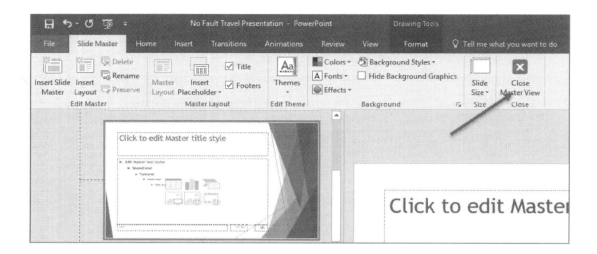

8. **Display the Side Master tab and then click the Close Master View tool on the ribbon to return to the Normal View.**

Scroll through your presentation to verify the changes you made, color scheme and slide number size appear on the existing slides.

### Saving a modified theme

If, after modifying a theme through the master slide view, you determine it is one you would like to use again, you can save it and use it again with other presentations. We will assume this is the case for these modifications. In this portion of the lesson you will save this modified theme and then apply it to a new presentation.

1. **Display the Design tab and then click the More arrow in the Themes group.**

## 2. After displaying all available themes, click Save Current Theme.

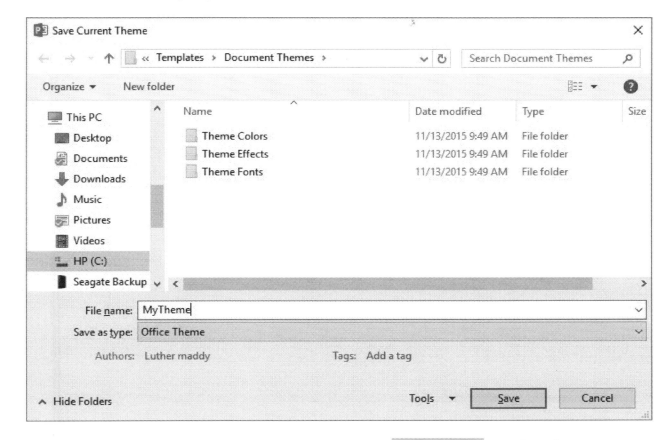

## 3. In the Save Theme dialog box, type *My Theme* as the theme name and click Save.

This new theme will now be available in the list of themes on this computer. You can apply it to new or existing presentations. You will now apply this new theme to a new presentation.

## 4. Save and close the No Fault Travel presentation.

---

**5.    Open the file menu and choose New.  Then select Blank Presentation.**

You have now started a new presentation using the "Blank" theme.  You will now apply the new theme, My Theme, you just created to this new presentation.

**6.    In the new presentation, click the Design tab and then the More drop down arrow in the Themes group.**

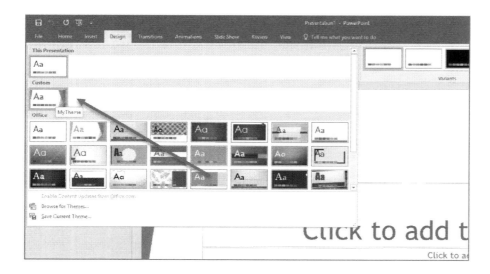

You should now see *My Theme* in the custom theme group. You can find the name of a theme by hovering the mouse over it.

**7.    Select My Theme from the Custom group to apply that theme to this slide presentation.**

**8.** **Insert three additional blank slides to this presentation. Use a different slide layout for each slide.**

All the new slides in this presentation should reflect the theme you created.

You may notice the slide numbers do not appear on the new slides. You can easily turn on the slide numbers using the Header and Footer tool on the Insert menu. This option is not saved with the theme. However, when you turn on the slide number option, they will have the formatting options you selected on the master slide, which in this case was a larger font size. If you wanted to have headers and footers appear with a new presentation you could create a presentation template, but we will save creating and using presentation templates for a more advanced course.

**9.** **Close the new presentation without saving.**

# Lesson #5: Working with Shapes

**In this lesson you will learn to:**
- o *Insert and Modify Shapes*
- o *Group Objects*
- o *Merge Shapes*

## Lesson #5:  Working with Shapes

### *Inserting Shapes*

PowerPoint makes it very easy to add shapes to your presentations.  These shapes can range from simple lines and arrows to callouts, stars and banners, and math symbols.  In this lesson you will insert shapes into your presentation.  You will also learn to add text to shapes as well as size and format those shapes.  You will then learn to combine shapes for copying, moving, and sizing with the Group option.

You will find the shapes available in the Illustrations group in the Insert tab.

**1.      Open the *No Fault Travel* presentation.**

**2.      Go to Slide #2 titled *We Specialize In.***

You will now add shapes to this slide to improve its appearance.

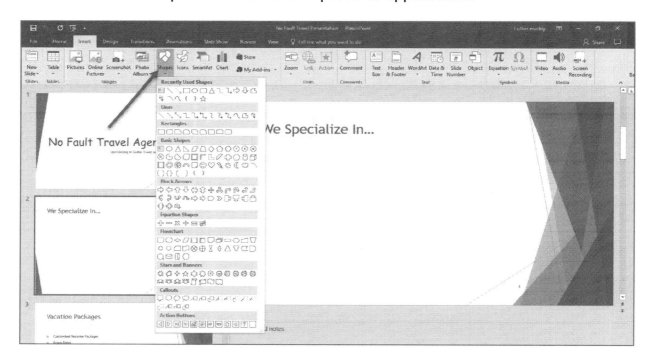

**3.      Display the View tab and ensure the Ruler option is selected.**

## 4. Display the Insert tab and click the Shapes tool.

You will now see the shapes available to insert into this slide. You should notice that PowerPoint arranges the shapes into groups of similar shapes.

## 5. In the list of shapes, choose the first rectangle shape on the left.

To create a shape you will first select the shape you wish to insert. Next, move the mouse pointer to the starting location. Then you can click and drag to specify the size of the shape you are creating.

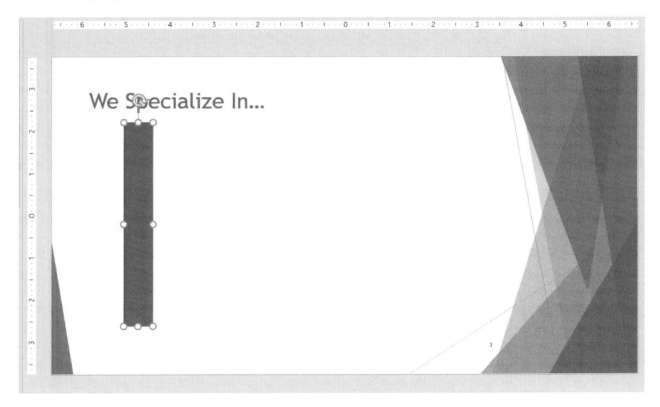

## 6. Using the horizontal and vertical rulers as a guide, click and drag to draw a rectangular shape about 5" long and 1/2" wide near the left side of the slide as shown.

If you do not get the shape exactly right the first time, you can use the sizing handles (the white shapes around the object) to re-size and move the object. Or, you can simply delete it and draw it again.

## 7. Click the Shapes tool again and locate the Block Arrows group.

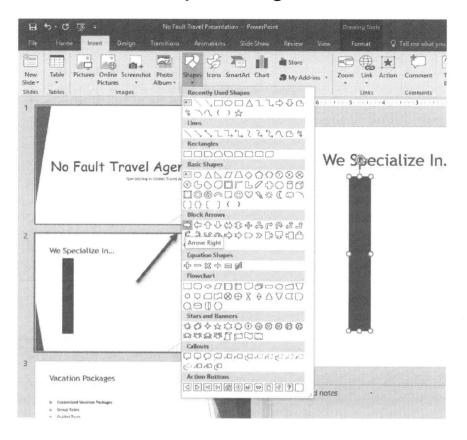

## 8. Choose the Right arrow in the Block Arrows group.

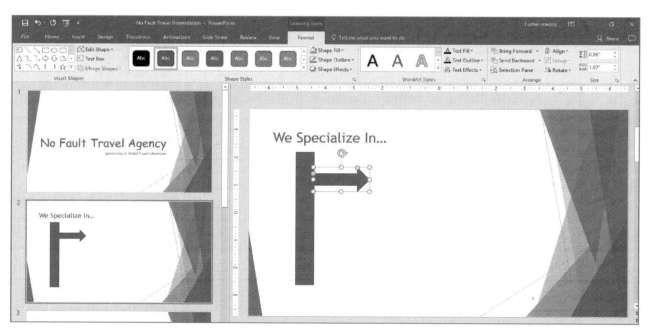

## 8. Click and drag to create an arrow that appears similar to the example.

### Insert Text in AutoShapes

Now you will add some text to the arrow you just created on this slide. To do this, you will right-click on the shape and then choose Edit Text from the shortcut menu.

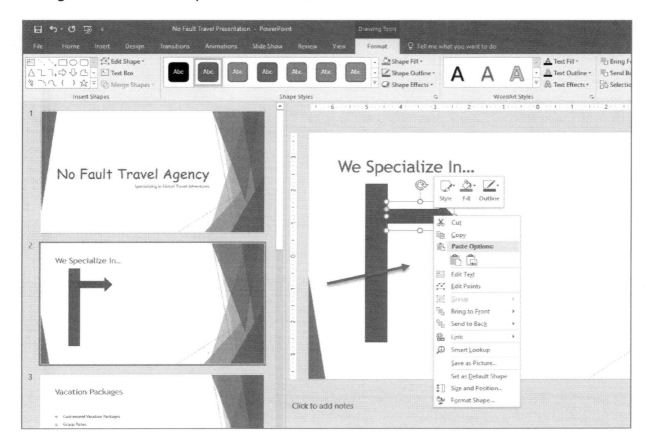

## 1. Right-click the arrow you just created. Then click Edit Text from the shortcut menu.

You should now see the cursor (insertion point) blinking in the arrow that is now functioning as a textbox. Now you can type the text you want in this shape and even apply font attributes to it.

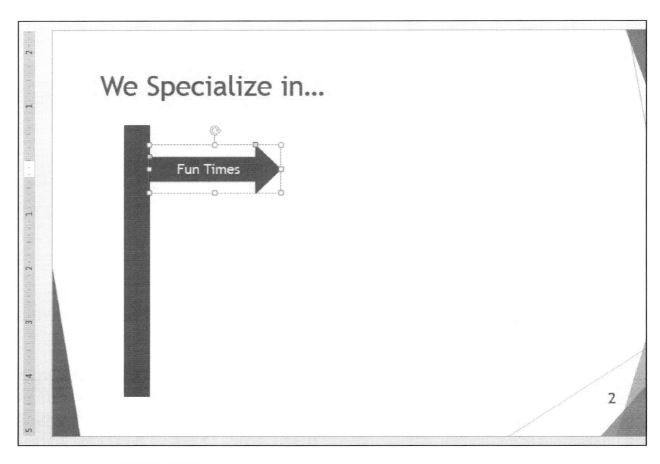

**2.** **Type *Fun Times* in the arrow.**

## Modifying Shapes

After creating a shape, you can modify the object by changing its fill color or pattern, line size and color, and text colors. PowerPoint allows you to apply formatting options on your own or choose from several pre-defined shape styles. In this portion of the lesson you will change some formatting options of the shapes you just created using pre-defined shape styles.

**1.** **Click on the rectangular object (the sign post) to select it.**

The sizing handles will display when the object is selected.

**2.** **Display the Drawing Tools Format tab if necessary, then Click the more down arrow in the Shape Styles group to display the pre-defined styles.**

The colors you see now match the theme's color scheme.

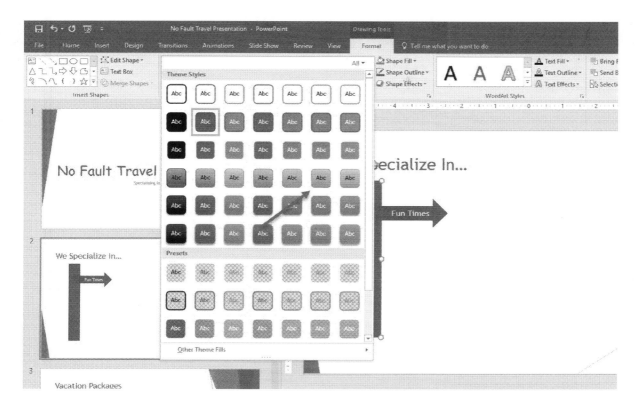

You will now see several pre-defined shape styles. These styles are tied to the color scheme of the theme you are using with the presentation.

### 3.     Choose the Intense Effect – Teal, Accent 5 color style.

### 4.     Select the arrow shape and apply the same color.

Both shapes should now have the color style you selected.

Now you will add a shape effect to the arrow you created.

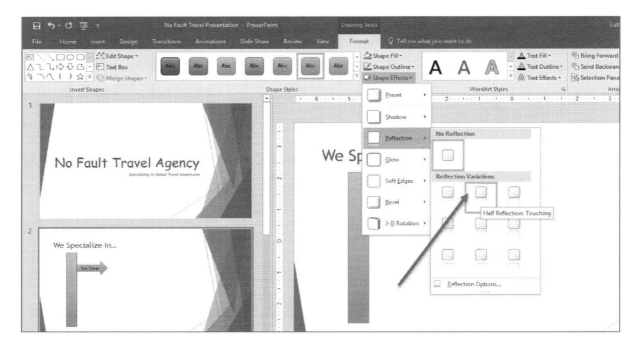

5. **With the arrow still selected, click the Shape Effects tool on the Format tab.**

6. **From the list of shape effects, choose Reflection and then Half Reflection, touching.**

You should now see this effect added to the arrow shape.

## Grouping Objects

Right now you have the sign you created consists of two separate shapes. If you wanted to move or copy the sign to another slide you would have to be sure you selected both objects when you cut or copied.

Grouping objects allows you to treat them as one object. This ensures you will get all the objects when you move or copy. Grouping the objects also allows you to size all the grouped shapes as if there were one object.

You will now group the two shapes you just created into one object.

1. **Click on the rectangular object to select it.**

2. **Now hold down the (Shift) key and click on the arrow object to select it also.**

---

You should now see sizing handles around both objects. This shows you that you are working with both shapes. The next step is to inform PowerPoint that you want to group these two shapes together.

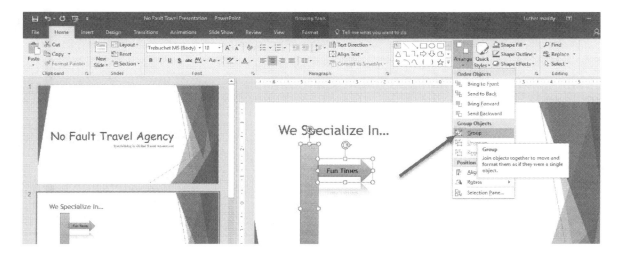

**3.    Keep the Format tab displayed and then click the Arrange tool and then choose Group.**

After you selected the Group option you should notice only one set of sizing handles around both shapes. The two shapes are now grouped and can be moved, copied, and sized as one object.

You will now copy this grouped shape to another slide.

**4.    Ensure the grouped shape is selected and then click the Copy tool on the Home tab.**

**5.    Move to slide #3, Vacation Packages, and click the Paste tool.**

PowerPoint placed this object in the same position it was on the prevoius slide. In this case, that positon blocks some of the slide's text. You will now move and rotate this object so it fits into this slide more appropriately.

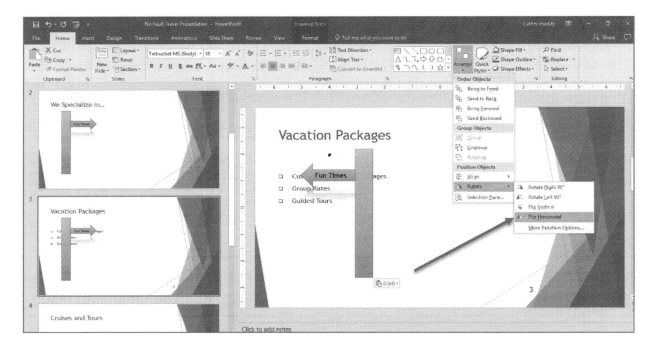

**6.** **With the object you just pasted still selected, click the Arrange tool on the Home tab. Then, choose Rotate and then Flip Horizontal.**

You can also use the Rotate tool in Format tab. The shape should now be flipped horizontally. You will now move this shape to the right side of the slide.

**7.** **Drag the shape to the right side of this slide.**

Your slide should appear similar to the example on the next page.

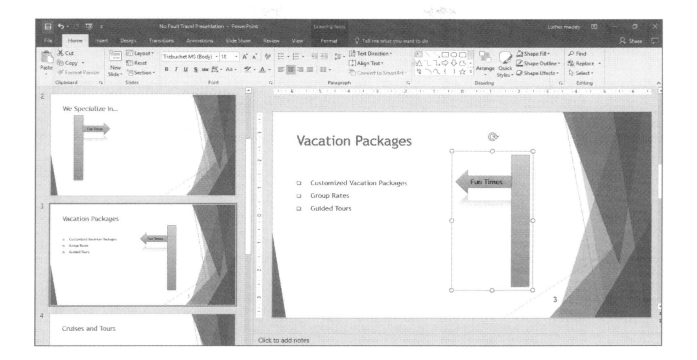

## Merging Shapes

With the group command you just used you, essentially turned two shapes into one. With the group command, each shape kept its own shape. The merge command will not only group shapes, but it will combine them in different ways to create entirely new shapes. In this portion of the lesson you will use the Union command that will combine several shapes into one, completely new and different shape.

This lesson will guide you through creating a cloud using several Oval shapes. If your shape does not end up exactly as the example, it will not matter.

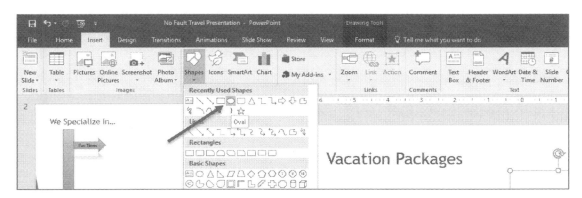

1.  **Remaining on the Vacation Packages slide, #3, select the Oval Shape from the Insert tab.**

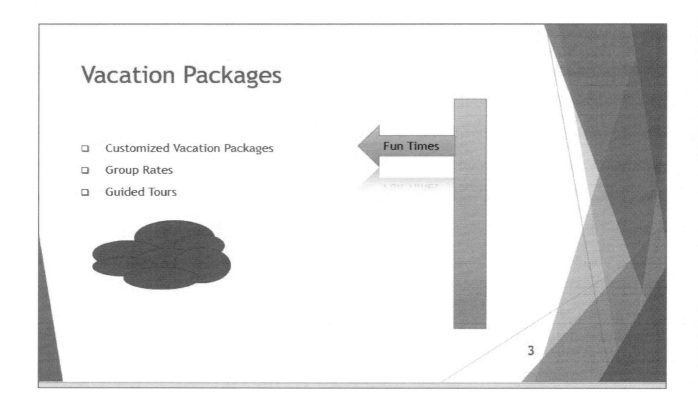

## 2. Use the Oval tool repeatedly to create a shape similar to that shown.

The example shape is created with seven ovals. After drawing an oval you can move and size it as needed to get the desired shape.

Now you will merge the seven ovals into a new shape. To do this you must first select all seven oval shapes. You can do this by clicking on each shape, holding the (Shift) key down after selecting the first one. Or, you can move above all the ovals and click and drag around the entire shape.

## 3. Click on one of the oval shapes. Then, hold the (Shift) key down and click the remaining six ovals.

You will know you have done this correctly when you see sizing handles and the selection outline for all seven shapes as shown.

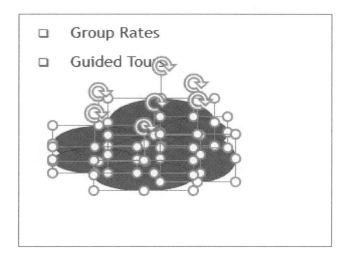

If you have trouble getting all seven shapes selected, try clicking and dragging around all the shapes to select them.

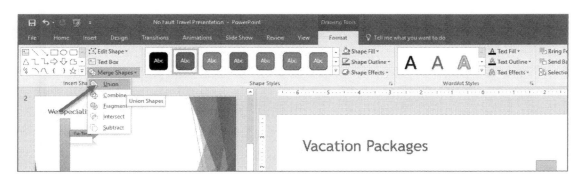

**4.      With all the ovals selected, click the Format tab in Drawing Tools and then click the Merge Shapes drop down arrow, then choose Union.**

PowerPoint will now combine all seven ovals into a new shape that hopefully, with a little imagination, resembles a cloud.  Now you will change the color of this new shape and add some text within it.

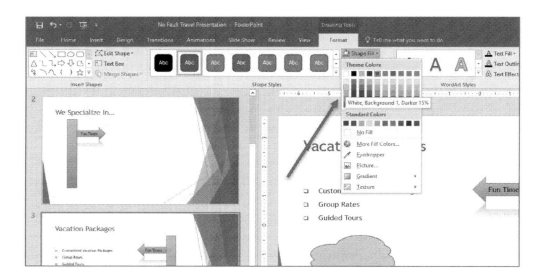

**5.** **With the cloud shape still selected, click the Shape fill tool on the Format tab and choose White, Background 1, Darker 15%.**

The cloud shape should have changed colors. You will now add text to this cloud.

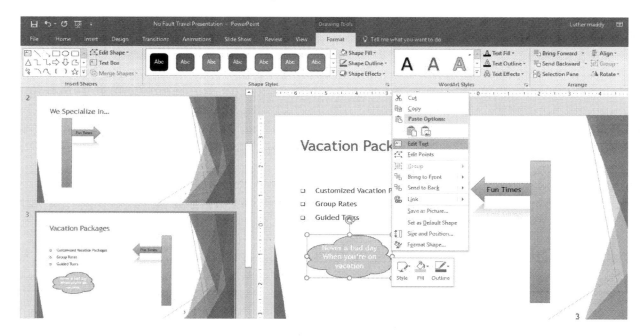

**6.** **Right-click the cloud and choose Edit Text from the shortcut menu. Type *Never a bad day* and press (Enter). Then on the next line type *when you're on vacation*.**

The text defaults to white. It will be easier for your audience to see if it is a darker color.

7. **While you are still in text editing mode, click and drag to select the text you just type and then change the font to a darker color.**

You can find the font color tool on the Home tab.

You can also adjust the size of the cloud shape to have the text fit as you desire.

There are several other features available on the Marge Shapes menu. Experiment with these on your own and exercise some creativity.

8. **Save and close the presentation.**

# Lesson #6: Inserting Pictures, Audio, and Video

**In this lesson you will learn to:**
- *Insert Pictures*
  - *Format Pictures*
- *Insert WordArt*
- *Insert Audio*
- *Insert Video*

## Lesson #6: Inserting Pictures, Audio, and Video

Adding pictures, sound, and even video clips to your presentations can make them very effective for some applications. You can simply dress up your presentations by adding images, or even bring in audio or video clips that enhance your message. Inserting these elements into your presentation is very easy. In this lesson you will begin by using the WordArt feature to add graphic text to the presentation. Next, you will add pictures, audio, and video clips.

**1.      Open the *No Fault Travel* presentation.**

You will now insert WordArt into a slide. WordArt is treated as an object, not text. It is important to spell it correctly when creating it because the spell checker will not display it as a misspelled word.

**2.      Press (Page Down) to go to Slide #2 titled *We Specialize In.***

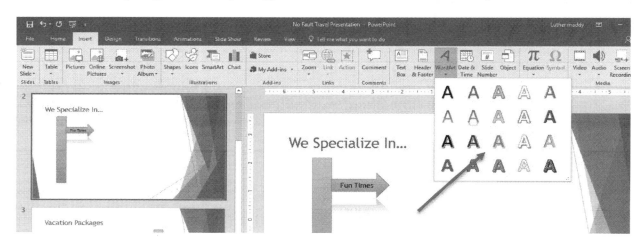

**3.      Display the Insert tab and then click the WordArt tool in the Text group.**

You will now see the WordArt Gallery that displays several WordArt styles to choose from.

**4.      In the WordArt Gallery select the third style down in the third column.**

PowerPoint will now insert a WordArt box. Here you can type the text you want as WordArt and then size or move this WordArt object.

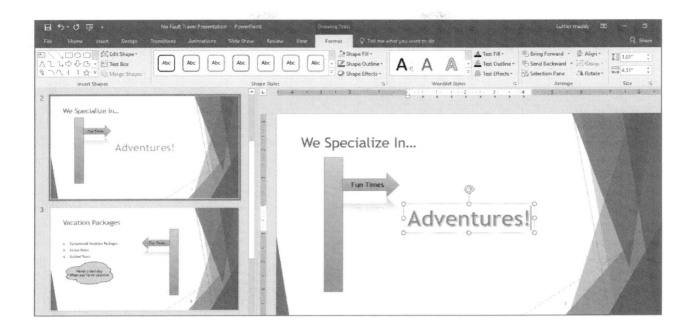

## 5. In the WordArt Text dialog box type *Adventures!*

You can now move and rotate the WordArt image as you see fit. You can also easily change the WordArt style by selecting another style from the WordArt Gallery when the WordArt image is selected.

## 6. Drag the WordArt object to the top middle of the slide as shown below.

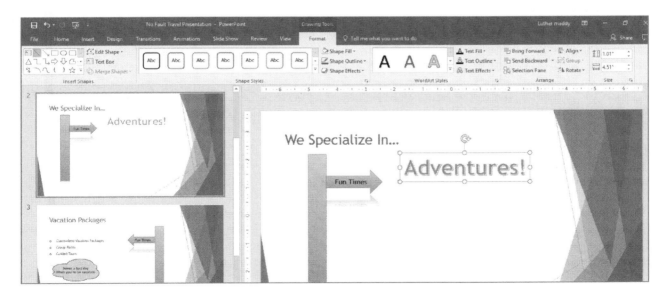

## Inserting clipart

With PowerPoint 2016 Microsoft has elected to have images stored online rather than installed with Microsoft Office. You can download pictures from a search engine, digital photographs, or images you have created yourself.

As you insert images from the Internet into your presentations, you should pay attention to the license that comes with the image. Bing.com will let you search images by license type. You can also find some public domain images on the author's website: http://www.LutherMaddy.com/?page_id=329

Downloading files from that site will be covered later in this lesson. For now, you can navigate to that site if you like and copy an image by right-clicking and choosing Copy from the shortcut menu.

Once you find an image on the Internet, and have verified the license is acceptable, you can simply use Copy and Paste to insert the image into your presentation.

You will now insert a picture into a slide.

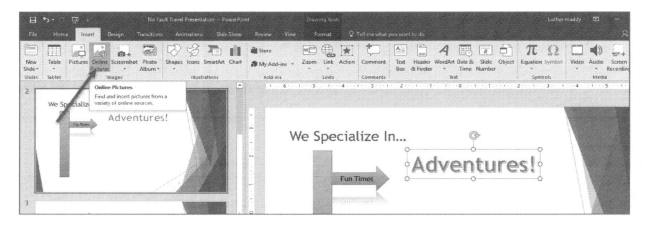

1. **Remaining on Slide #2, display the Insert Tab and then click the Online Pictures tool.**

After clicking the Online Pictures tool you should see the Insert Pictures dialog box. Here you will enter a topic in the search box to display images that match your search criteria.

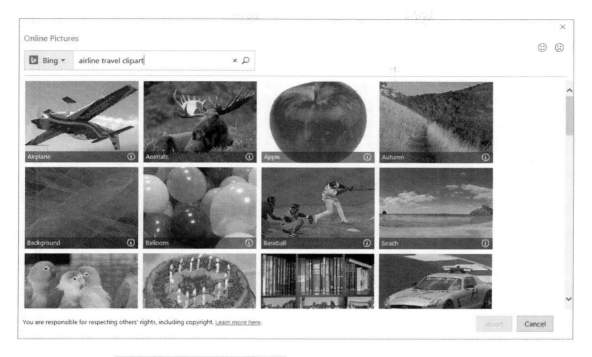

**2.** **Type *airline travel clipart* in the Search textbox in the Online Pictures dialog box and press (Enter).**

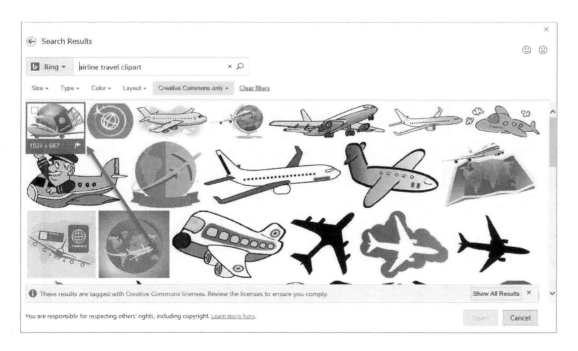

Bing will now display images related to your search text, airline travel. When you see an image you like, just click on it to insert it into the slide.

**3.** **Click on an image similar to that shown and then click Insert.**

After inserting an image you can size and move it as you see fit.

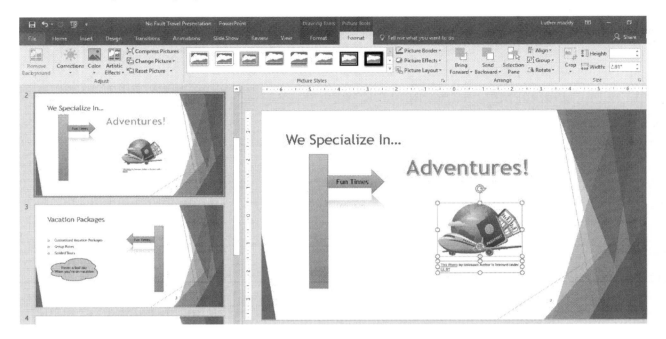

# 4. Position and size the image so it appears similar to the example.

## Modify clipart

PowerPoint allows you to make minor changes to Clip Art images. For example, you can change the colors displayed in the image. You can also select picture styles that add borders and change its shape. You can do this using the Format Tab when the picture is selected.

You will now modify the Clip Art you just inserted.

1. **Select the image you just inserted, then ensure the Format Tab is displayed.**

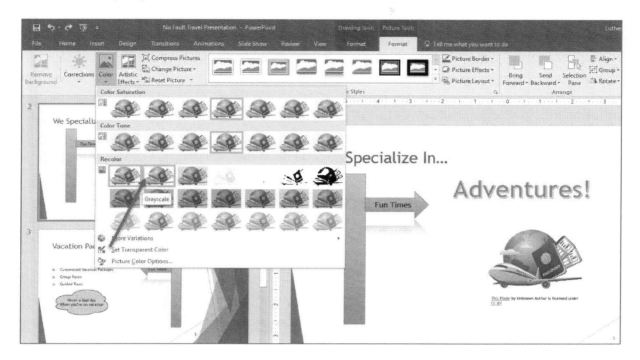

2. **Click the Color tool on the Format tab.**

PowerPoint will now show you several color options you can choose for this image.

3. **Select Grayscale from the color choices in the Recolor Options section.**

You can experiment with different colorations as you like. There are many formatting options available for the images you insert into PowerPoint slides. Take your time and experiment with these as you are creating your own presentations. In this portion of the lesson you will apply a picture style to the image.

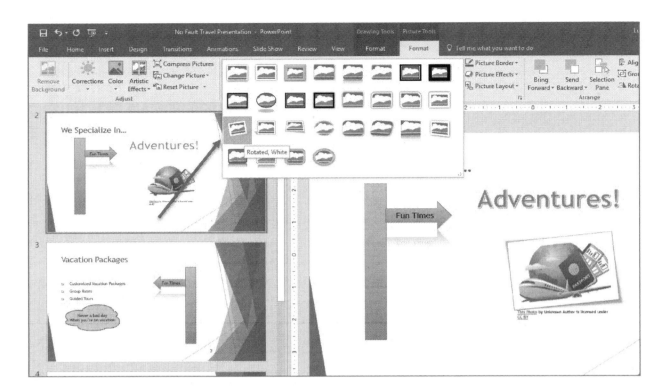

**4.** **Click the more drop down button for Picture styles and choose Rotated White.**

The image will now be formatted with the picture style you selected.

> **Presentation tip:** While graphic images, sounds, and video clips seem to liven up a presentation, they can also be a distraction. Ensure that any images and other enhancements you add to your presentations do not diminish its impact by attracting more attention than the message you are trying to communicate.

## Inserting Audio files

You can insert sounds, music, and videos that are available in the Clip Organizer or files stored on your computer. To insert audio and video, you will use the Insert Tab. In addition to the media available on your computer, you can also download additional sounds, and videos from the Internet. In order to play sounds, you need speakers and a sound card on your computer. If you do not have speakers or headphones installed, PowerPoint may not allow you to insert audio into your presentations.

You can also record your own sounds or a voice narration if you have a microphone connected to your computer.

In addition to these options, you can also create hyperlinks to videos on the Internet such as YouTube. In this portion of the lesson you will insert audio and video clips and create a hyperlink to a YouTube video.

---

### Downloading media files

Because computers vary in the media installed on them, this workbook will have you download media from the author's website. It is not necessary that you do this, but the workbook will reference the files on this website in the exercises. If you choose not to download the files referenced here, or prefer to use you own files, you may do so. Just remember that your file names and location may be different than that referenced in the lesson.

The steps for downloading the files referenced in the remaining portion of this lesson are as follows:

1.      **In your Internet browser, go to:**
        **http://www.LutherMaddy.com/?page_id=329**

On this page you will find clipart, audio, and video files that you can download to your computer.

You will now download two audio files and one video file to use in this lesson. The first file you will download is the Sunshine audio file.

**2.     Click the word *Sunshine* to the right of the word Download.**

Depending on the Internet browser you are using, you may see the Save As dialog box. Here you will navigate to the folder where you want to have this file and specify a name if you want to name the file something other than Sunshine.

If your browser or operating system does not ask you where to save the files you are downloading, you will most likely find them in the Downloads folder. Your browser may list these files at the bottom of the window. If so, you can click the arrow to the right of the name and select "Show in Folder" to learn where the files were downloaded.

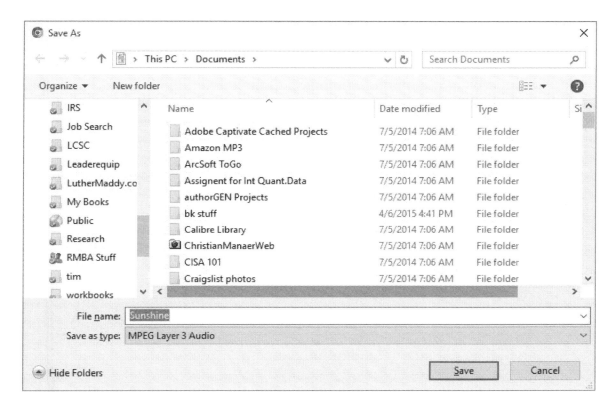

3.  **If you see the Save As dialog box navigate to the Documents Folder. Leave the file name as Sunshine and click Save.**

The Documents folder is not where you would normally save media files. However, for instructional purposes, placing the media files here will make them easier to find and delete when you no longer need them.

**4.** **Repeat this process to download the audio file *Water* and the video file *Lake*. Save to the documents folder or move them there, after they have downloaded.**

The video file may take several seconds to download.

You now have three media files to use in the remaining portion of this lesson.

___

You will insert an audio file on the first slide of this presentation.

**1.** **Ensure you are viewing the first slide in the No Fault Travel presentation. On the Insert tab, click the Audio tool, then choose Audio on my PC.**

You will now see the Insert Audio dialog box. Here you will navigate to the folder that contains the audio file you want to insert and, for example purposes, that will be the Documents folder. The files you downloaded may be in the Downloads folder.

2. **Navigate to the Documents, or Downloads folder. Then, select the Sunshine file and then click Insert.**

PowerPoint should have inserted a speaker icon and playback bar inserted on the first slide. This is the audio object. You will also set Playback options that will control when the audio plays and for how long.

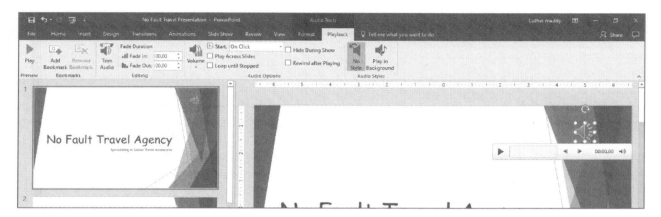

3. **Drag the audio icon to the top right corner of the slide and then display the Playback tab.**

You have moved the audio icon to a less conspicuous location on the slide.

The Sunshine audio clip will be used for background music on the first slide. You will instruct PowerPoint to continue playing this clip until you advance to the next slide. PowerPoint 2016 does allow you to play sounds through multiple slides with the Play in Background or Play Across Slides options. In this case you want this sound to play only while the first slide is displayed.

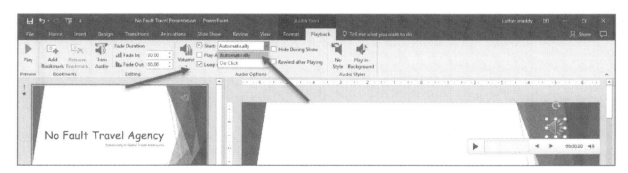

4. **In the Audio Options group in the Playback tab, click the Start drop down list and choose Automatically. Also, click turn on the Loop until Stopped checkbox.**

You have informed PowerPoint to start playing this audio clip as soon as the slide show starts. It will continue to play until you stop it by advancing to the second slide.

**5.    Now move to slide #4, Cruises and Tours, and insert the audio file named *Water*.**

Remember, you can use your own audio files in this lesson if you choose.

**6.    Move the audio object (speaker icon) to the bottom right corner. Then, in the Playback tab, choose Automatically for the start and also turn on the Loop until Stopped check box in the Audio Options group.**

As with the first audio clip you inserted, this clip will also play as soon as this slide is displayed and continue playing until you move to the next slide.

You will hear these clips at the end of this lesson.

### Inserting Videos in Presentations

If you have a video clip saved as a file, such as the Lake file downloaded earlier in the lesson, you can embed it directly into a presentation. You can have the video play as the slide appears or when you click on it.

If you want to use a video online, such as one on YouTube, you can create a hyperlink in your presentation. When you are viewing a presentation with a hyperlink, clicking the link will start the computer's browser and play the video. When the video completes, closing the browser will return to the presentation. In this portion of the lesson you will embed the Lake video directly into a slide. You will also create a hyperlink to a YouTube video.

You will add a new slide to this presentation and embed the Lake video into it.

**1.    Move to the last slide in the presentation and click the New Slide tool on the Home tab.**

PowerPoint should choose the Title and Content layout and that is exactly what you need for this video. If needed, change the slide layout.

**2.    Click in the Title placeholder and type *It's time for a relaxing vacation!***

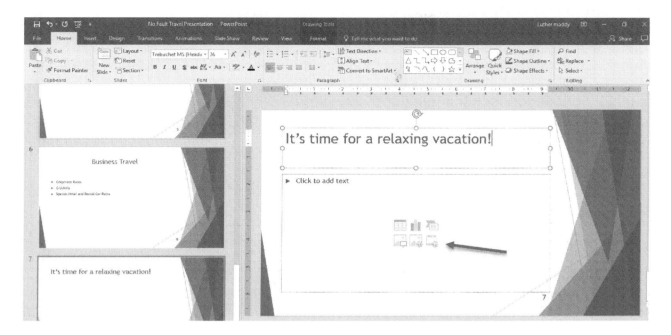

The Title and content slide allows you to easily insert a video clip by clicking the video icon in this slide.

## 3.    Click the Insert Video icon on this new slide.

You will now see the Insert Video dialog box. Here you will navigate to the folder that contains the video you want to insert.

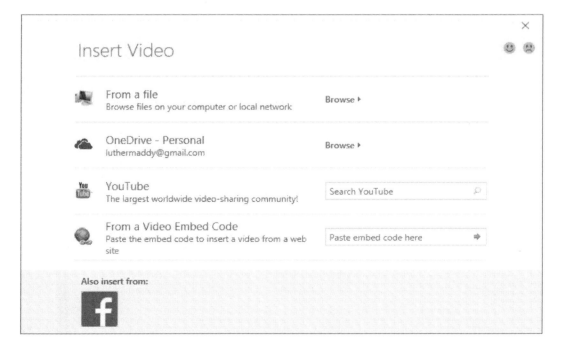

**4.    In the Insert Video dialog box, click Browse in the From a file section.**

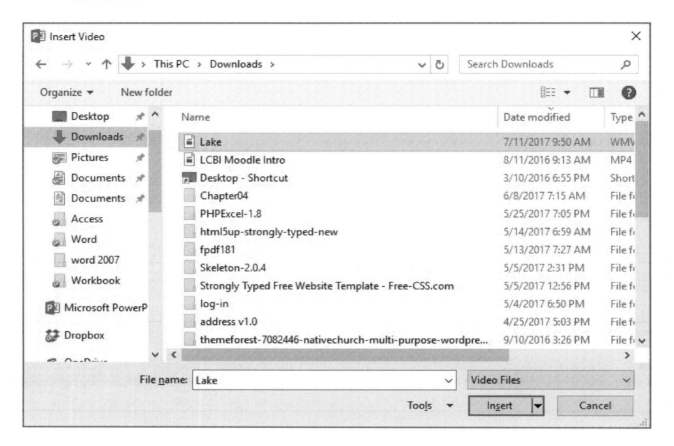

**5.    Navigate to the Documents or Downloads folder, select the Lake video file, and then click Insert.**

After inserting the video clip you can set the Playback options to tell PowerPoint when to play this video. In this case, you will leave the default options, which means the video will only play when you click on it during the presentation.

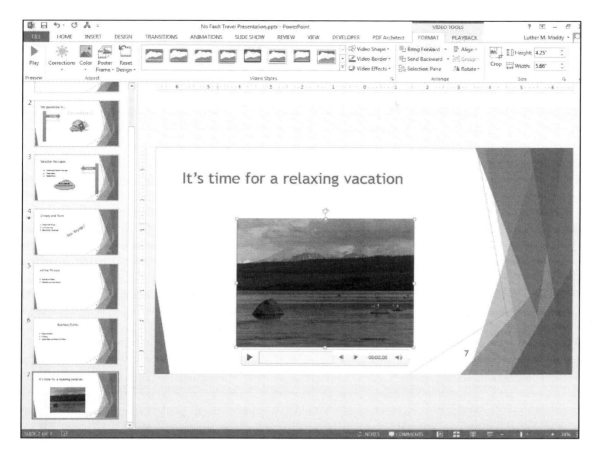

You will now insert a new slide and create a hyperlink on that slide to a YouTube video. The exercise will give you an address to a video, but since the Internet is ever changing, the link may no longer work. In that case, you can find another video on YouTube that you wish to include in the presentation.

**6.   On the Home tab, click the New Slide tool again to insert another Title and Content slide after the slide with the video.**

**7.   Click in the Title placeholder of this slide and type *How about a cruise?***

To create a hyperlink you will link some portion of text on the slide to the video on the Internet you want to view when the text is clicked. Hyperlinks only work when you are in presentation mode. In this portion of the exercise you will link the title you just created to a YouTube video.

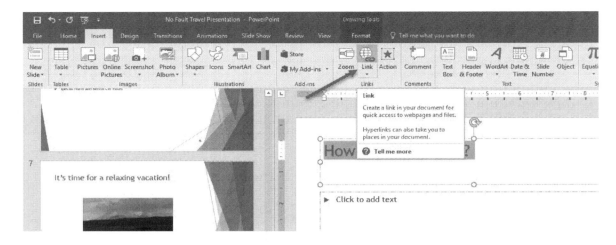

**8.** **Click and drag to select the title in the slide you just created, then click the Link tool on the Insert tab.**

PowerPoint will now display the Insert Hyperlink dialog box. Here you will specify the location, web address in this case, you want to jump to when this text is clicked while the presentation is being displayed.

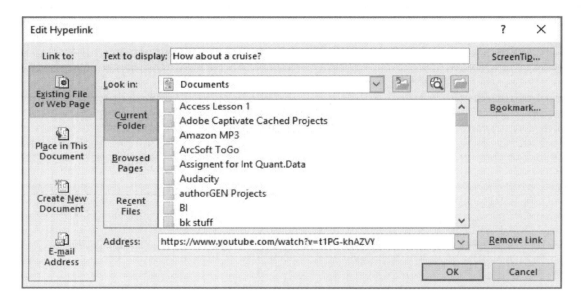

**9.** **In the Insert Hyperlink dialog box, ensure the Existing File or Web Page option is selected, then type *Https://www.youtube.com/watch?v=t1PG-khAZVY* in the Address area.**

Because the web is fluid, web addresses may change. If this link does not work, find one you like on YouTube.

The Web address in this step is case sensitive and since pages on the Internet change often, it may not be correct when you are completing this less.

When you are linking to YouTube videos you have located yourself, you can copy the address from the browser and paste it into this dialog box. Web addresses can be very difficult to type and copying them directly from the address bar ensures they are correct.

## 10. Click OK in the Insert Hyperlink dialog box after typing the address.

If you click away from the title textbox you should notice that PowerPoint changed the color of the title and added underlining. This is how this presentation theme displays hyperlinks.

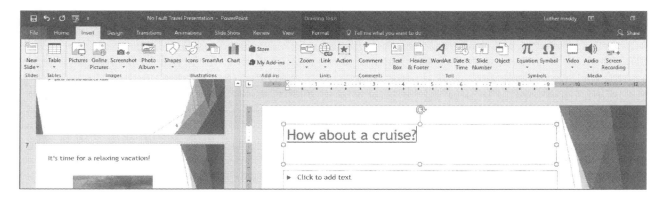

**Presentation tip:** If you do use website hyperlinks in your presentations, it is a good idea to verify they work correctly, just before starting your presentation. You don't want to be caught off guard.

Clicking on the hyperlink will do nothing at this point. As we previously mentioned, the presentation must be running for the link to work.

You are now ready to run this presentation and see the audio, video, and hyperlink in action.

## 11. Save the presentation and then start the slide show from the beginning. You can do this from the Slide Show tab.

As you run the slide show, notice the audio plays on the first slide until you advance to the next slide. Advance through the show. Be sure to click on the Lake video and Cruise hyperlink. Close the browser after viewing the YouTube video to return to the presentation.

**12. End the presentation and return to PowerPoint's editing mode.**

### *Inserting screenshots into presentations*

Sometimes you will want to add a graphic image directly from your computer to your PowerPoint presentation. Inserting screenshots has many uses. For example, you may be conducting a training session in which you need to reference a screen from a software package. Or, you may want to reference a website in your presentation.

Regardless of your use, inserting a screen into a presentation is very easy. To insert a screenshot into a PowerPoint slide you will first find and display the page you want to insert. Then you will use the Screenshot tool on the Insert tab to place the screenshot in the slide.

In this portion of the lesson, you will insert a screenshot from a travel related website into the No Fault Travel presentation. PowerPoint also allows you to record and insert screen recordings. For this lesson, you will just capture an image.

**1. In Normal View, move to the last slide by pressing the (End) key. Then insert a new Title and Content slide.**

Remember, the Title and Content layout is selected by default and you can simply click the new slide icon.

**2. In the new slide, click in the Title placeholder and type *Stay informed with travel advisories*.**

Now you will need to locate the screen you want to insert into this slide. For example purposes this lesson references the United States government's travel advisory website. You can use any screen you wish, or follow along with these specific instructions.

**3. Minimize PowerPoint and start your computer's Internet browser.**

**4. Go to *http://travel.state.gov/content/passports/english/alertswarnings.html***

You can also find this site by typing *United States travel warnings and alerts* in a search engine. This saves possible errors in typing the exact address.

**5. After locating the correct internet page, minimize the browser and return to PowerPoint.**

You will now use the Insert Screenshot tool to insert an image of the travel advisory site into this slide.

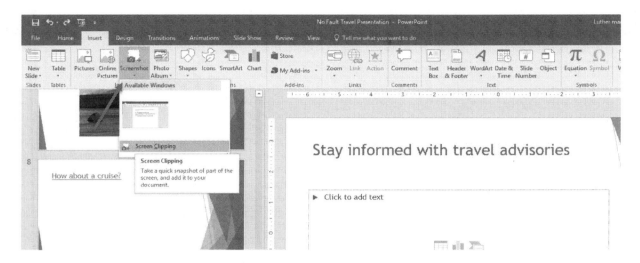

## 5.   Click the Screenshot tool on the Insert tab.

You may see a thumbnail of the travel alerts site.  If so, you may simply click on it to insert it.  The next steps in this exercise will have you capture a portion of a screen using the Screen Clipping feature.

## 6.   Click the Screen Clipping option.

PowerPoint should now minimize and the browser window with the Travel Advisory site should be available.

## 7.   Click and drag to select the portion of the screen you want to insert into the PowerPoint slide.

When you release the mouse, you will be returned to PowerPoint and the image will appear in the slide.

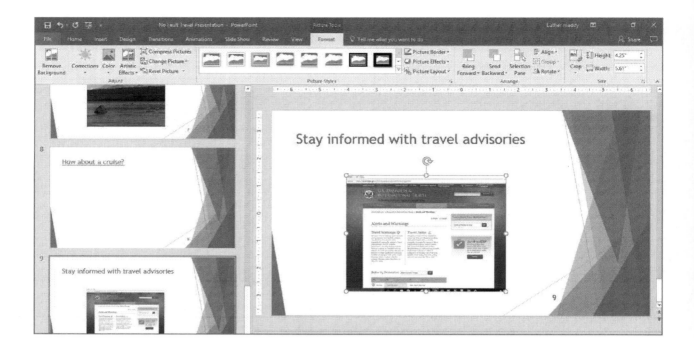

Stretch out the image to make it fit the slide.

## 5.    Save and close this presentation.

# Lesson #7:  Building and Running Slide Shows

## In this lesson you will learn to:
- o Add slide transitions
- o Annotate slide shows
- o Use the mouse as a laser pointer

# Lesson #7: Building and Running Slide Shows

## Slide transition effects

When you played this slide show in earlier lessons, the slides simply disappear and appear as you advance to the next slide. PowerPoint allows you to add transition effects between the slides. Slide transition effects can make your presentations more interesting and eye-catching. There are several transitions available and in this lesson you will explore some of them.

> **Presentation tip:** Slide transitions can provide a visual stimulus between the slides, but can also distract your audience. Use them carefully.

## 1.      Open the *No Fault Travel* presentation.

You will now switch to the Slide Sorter view. This view is very effective for adding slide transitions, especially when you want to apply different transitions within the presentation, which is probably more appropriate for a classroom setting than it is for a "real" presentation.

## 2.      Click Slide Sorter on the View tab.

## 3.      Once in Slide Sorter view click the Transitions Tab.

Here you will see many transition affects you can add to one slide or all the slides. There are more transitions available than you can see on the ribbon. Like other features you have used with PowerPoint, there is a "more" drop down arrow. Clicking this arrow will display all of the transition effects available.

In the Slide Sorter view you should notice that the first slide has an orange border around it, indicating it is the selected slide. You should recall working with the Slide Sorter View in an earlier lesson.

If you click on a transition effect on the ribbon, PowerPoint will give you a preview of that transition on the selected slide. This allows you to easily explore the various transitions available in PowerPoint. Switching to Normal View will give you an even larger preview of the slide transition.

For exploration purposes, you will now choose different transition effects for each slide.

4.    **With the first slide selected, click the More drop down button to display the entire list of transitions. Select the Glitter transition for this slide.**

As you selected the Glitter transition you should notice a preview of that transition on slide one. PowerPoint also allows you to specify how long the transition should last. You can adjust the transition during in the Duration textbox.

5.    **Change the Duration setting to 6:00 seconds. Then click the Preview tool at the far left.**

You should notice the transition effect slowed down and took longer from start to finish.

You will now set transition effects for each slide.

**6.    Click on slide #2 to select it.  Locate and apply the Honeycomb transition.**

**7.    Repeat the above process for each slide and apply the following transition effects:**

- Slide #3: Ferris Wheel
- Slide #4: Uncover
- Slide #5: Checkerboard
- Slide #6: Wind
- Slide #7: Clock
- Slide #8: Fracture
- Slide #9: Crush

You can also adjust the duration of the transitions on these slides if you wish.

After selecting a transition effect for a slide, you will see that PowerPoint has added a small icon below that slide indicating that slide has a transition effect.  You can click on that icon to preview the transition effect.

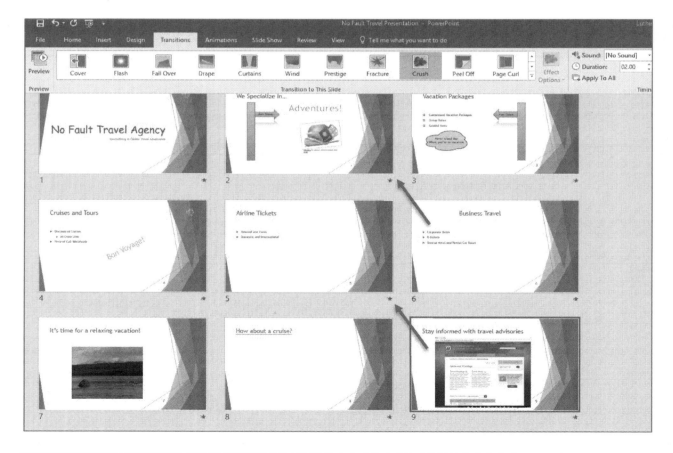

You will now run the slide show to see the transition effects in action on the full screen.

**8.    Display the Slide Show tab and click the From Beginning tool.**

As you displayed the first slide you should notice that the background music you applied did not start until the transition completed.

**9.    Press (Enter) or click the mouse to display the next slide.**

**10.   Continue advancing through the presentation until you return to PowerPoint's editing mode.**

You will notice that when the slide presentation concludes you will revert to the view you were in before you ran the slide show.  Since you were in Slide Sorter View when you started the presentation that is the view PowerPoint returned after the presentation completed.

### *Annotating slides with the pen*

It is possible to annotate or markup a slide while you are presenting the slide show. This is useful if you need to add extra emphasis somewhere in the slide while you are presenting the slide show.

After making annotations, PowerPoint will ask you if you want to make them a permanent part of the presentation.  If you elect to save them they will become graphic objects on the slide.   Even if you save the annotations, you can remove them later by selecting them with a mouse click and pressing (Delete).

You will now display a pen as you run the slide show and annotate a slide.

**1.    Start the Slide Show from the beginning.**

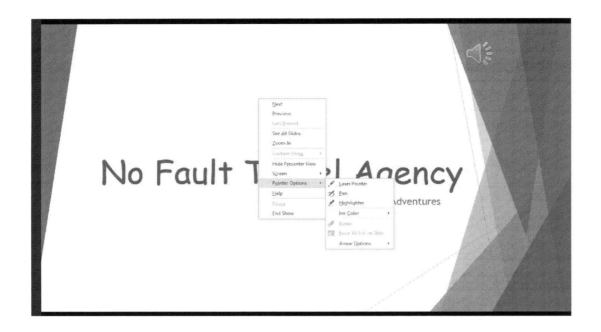

**2.    After the transition to this slide is completed, right-click somewhere in the slide.**

You should now see a shortcut menu of actions you can take while you are viewing the slide show. You will also notice the music stopped. You set this audio clip to run until stopped.  PowerPoint interprets your mouse click as a stop signal.

You will now tell PowerPoint you want to use your mouse pointer as a pen to annotate the slides while you are displaying them.

**3.    In the shortcut menu, choose Pointer Options, and then Pen.**

Now, as you click and drag, your mouse will draw lines wherever you move.  By default the pen color will be red.  You can change this by selecting the Ink Color option in the shortcut menu.

**4.    Now, click and drag the mouse to underline the word Adventures at the bottom of the slide. Then try drawing an arrow pointing to that word as shown in the example.**

If you are artistically or mouse challenged, don't worry, you can press (E) to quickly erase your pen marks, and start over.

When you are done annotating the slide you can right-click and switch the pointer back to an arrow. Or, you can also quickly turn off the pen mode by pressing the escape (ESC) key. Be careful using the escape key because if you press it more than once, PowerPoint will the end presentation.

**5.    After annotating this slide, right-click to display the shortcut menu. Choose Pen again to turn off this option.**

You are now back in normal presentation mode. You may also notice the background music started again.

### Annotating slides with the highlighter

PowerPoint also has a highlighter option for annotating slides. It is similar to the pen but is thicker and appears as if you were highlighting text on paper. In this portion of the lesson you will use the highlighter to annotate a slide.

**1.    Advance the slide show until you arrive at the "Vacation Packages" slide.**

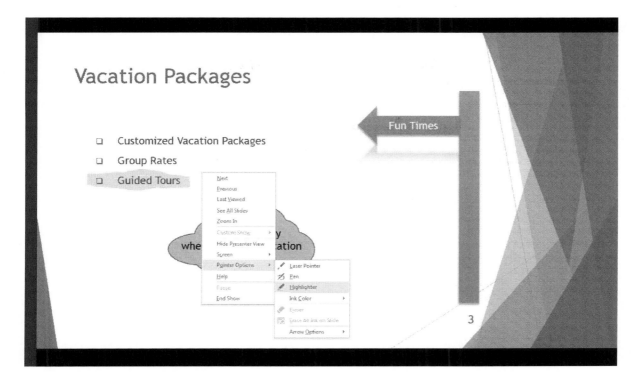

2. **Viewing this slide, right-click and choose Pointer Options and then Highlighter. Next, use the mouse to highlight the words, "Guided Tours", as shown.**

3. **After using the highlighter, right-click and change the mouse pointer back to an arrow by turning off the Highlighter.**

4. **Continue to advance slides until you complete the slide show.**

When you complete the slide show, PowerPoint will ask if you want to keep or discard the annotations you have made.

5. **When asked if you want to keep or discard the ink annotations, choose Keep.**

You will now be returned to Slide Sorter view. While examining the slides, you should see that your annotations have become part of the slides. If you now decide to remove them, you can easily delete annotations from the slide. You can do this by viewing the slide in Normal view and then selecting and deleting the annotation. You will delete the annotations you created earlier in this portion of the lesson.

1.   **In the Slide Sorter View, double click the first slide to view it in Normal view.**

2.   **Click on the red annotations to select them and press (Delete).**

Even though you drew two elements here, PowerPoint treated the annotation as one object.

3.   **View slide #3, Vacation Packages, in Normal view and delete the highlighting on this slide.**

## Using the mouse as a laser pointer

If you want to emphasize something while you are in presentation mode you can use the pen or highlighter as you have just seen. PowerPoint also allows you to change your mouse pointer into a "laser pointer". In actuality this simply changes the mouse pointer from an arrow into a red dot resembling a laser pointer.

Turning your mouse into a laser pointer is relatively simple, but it is a two handed operation. To turn the mouse pointer into a laser pointer, press and hold the (Control) key and then click and hold the left mouse button. As long as you hold down the (Control) key and the mouse button, the pointer will resemble a laser pointer.

You can also change the mouse pointer into a laser pointer by right-clicking and choosing Laser Pointer in the Pointer Options. This will change the mouse pointer until you turn in off with the right-click process.

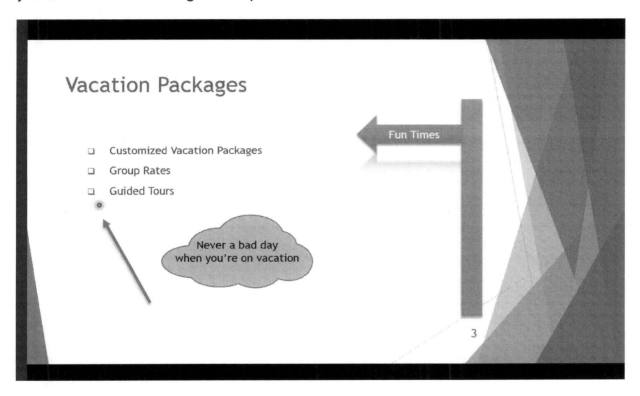

**Presentation tip:** If you do not want to be tied to your computer during presentations, consider purchasing a wireless presenter tool. These tools are very small and allow you to move from slide to slide. These devices are incorporate laser pointers. Wireless presenter mice are inexpensive and give you the freedom to move around the room during your presentation.

You have now seen several features you can add to your presentations to make them more attractive and informative. Experiment on your own because PowerPoint has many features we have not discussed in this course. If you want to learn even more about PowerPoint, consider taking the next level class.

**4.  Save and close the presentation.**

# Lesson #8: Printing Presentations

## In this lesson you will learn to:

- o *Print Slide Handouts*
- o *Print notes pages*
- o *Print in grayscale to save ink*

## Lesson #8: Printing Presentations

PowerPoint gives you several options and choices when you are ready to print. You can print an entire presentation, an outline the presentations, speaker notes and even audience handouts. You can print these in color, grayscale, or pure black and white.

In this lesson you will explore some of the printing features available in PowerPoint.

### *Printing in grayscale*

To save ink costs, when creating your presentation you may wish to print it in grayscale rather than color. In addition to printing, you can also view your presentation in gray scale. This allows you to see how your presentation will appear if printed in black and white or grayscale. This is helpful if you are producing many sets of audience handouts and elect to print them in black and white rather than color.

### 1.    Open the *No Fault Travel* presentation.

You will now view the presentation in black and white and grayscale.

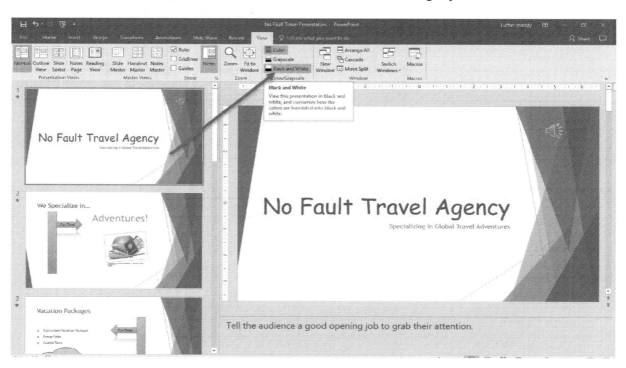

### 2.    Click the View tab, then choose Black and White.

After you select the Black and White view PowerPoint will add a Black And White tab. You can use this tab to quickly switch back to color view, or view variations of the Black and White view.

---

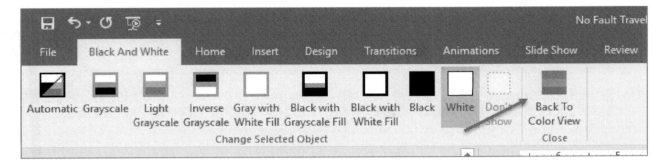

3. **After viewing some of the slides in Black and White, choose Back to Color from the Black and White tab. Then click Grayscale from the View tab.**

4. **Switch back to Color view.**

Now you will change the print options. This way you can keep your presentation View mode in color, but still be able to print in black and white or in grayscale.

5. **Click the File menu tab and choose print.**

In the backstage view, after choosing the print option, you can select the color options with the drop down.

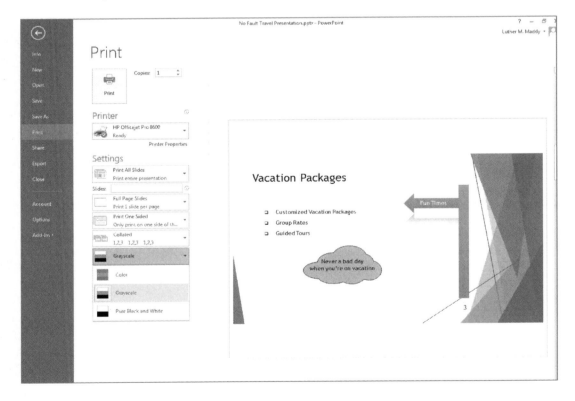

## 6. In the Print options Settings, click the Color drop down list and choose Grayscale.

You should notice that the print preview now displays in grayscale. This has not affected how your presentation will be displayed, only how it is printed. If you are not using a color printer, the color option will default to grayscale. The color option will not be available for printing.

As you examine this screen you will also notice you can choose which slides (pages) print. By default, all slides in your presentation will be printed unless you choose otherwise. To print only the current slide, selected slide, or a specific range of slides, you can click the down arrow in the section that currently displays "Print All Slides".

If you choose the Custom Range option, you can specify which slides you want to print, 1-5 for example.

### *Printing audience handouts*

PowerPoint allows you to print audience handouts in several variations. One of the most useful handout configurations places three slides on a page and also has an area for participants to take notes.  This is the option you will select in this portion of the lesson.

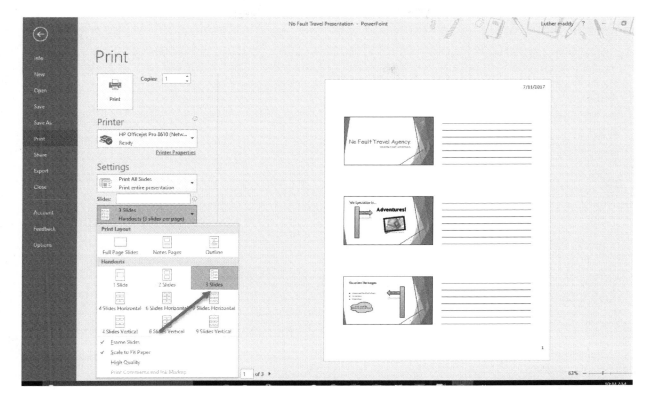

**1.  Click the slides drop down arrow and choose 3 Slides in the handouts group.**

After selecting this option, you will notice the preview displays how the handouts will appear when printed.  Each page has three slides and a notes area, as shown in the example.

To actually print the handouts you can simply click the Print button.

We left the color mode in grayscale.  If you have a color printer and wanted to print the handouts in color, you would just change back to color before printing.

### Printing speaker notes

You may recall adding one short note in the Notes area on slide one. These notes are primarily designed to serve as "index cards" for the presenter.  If you do add notes here to help you deliver your presentation, you can easily print a version of your presentation that displays those notes.

To print notes pages, you will choose that option from the Slides drop down list.

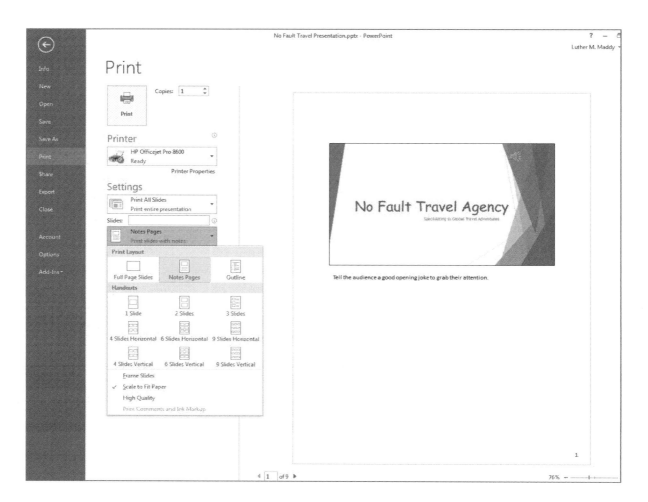

1.  **Switch back to color mode, if available. Then click the slides drop down arrow and choose Notes Pages in the Print Layout group.**

You should see a preview showing how the notes pages will appear when printed.

To save paper and ink, you can save actually printing for your real presentations. However, you have seen some of the options available to you when printing.

2.  **Press (Esc) to leave the Print menu and return to PowerPoint. Save and close the presentation.**

You could also click the Left, back arrow to leave the backstage view.

You have now completed a basic introduction to PowerPoint. You should be able to create impressive and useful presentations! Experiment with the many additional features PowerPoint and become even more effective in its use, and also consider taking a class that covers even more of PowerPoint's features.

# Index

# Other books that may interest you

## Excel: The Basics (2016, 2013, or 2010)
*In "learning by doing" you will gain a good grasp of the basics of Excel. You'll learn to create formulas, format and print worksheets, copy and move cell data, and generate attractive cha and graphs from your Excel data.*

2016: Retail price: $9.95    2010: Retail price: $8.95

## Excel: Beyond The Basics (2016, 2013, or 2010)
*In "learning by doing" you will gain a good grasp of the Excel features beyond the basic level You'll learn to create advanced formulas using Excel functions like PMT(), IF(), VLookup() ar more. You'll also learn about worksheet protection, data validation, creating and using templates, advanced charting features, and much more.*

Retail price:  $9.95

## Excel: Database and Statistical Features (2016, 2013, or 2010)
*In "learning by doing" you will gain a good grasp of the Excel database features. You'll learn create and use Pivot Tables and Charts. You'll also learn about database functions like DSum() and DAverage(). You'll also learn about filtering and subtotaling Excel data. Finally, you'll learn about performing statistical analysis using the Analysis Toolpak.*

Retail price:  $9.95

## Word: The Basics (2016, 2013, or 2010)
*In "learning by doing" you will learn the basics of MS Word. You'll also be introduced to performing tasks the most efficient way possible to increase your productivity. This workbook covers document creation and editing. You'll learn to copy and move and enhance text. You also learn about page a paragraph formatting, setting tabs, creating tables and more.*

2016: Retail price:  $9.95    2010: Retail price:  $8.95

## Word: Enhancing Documents (2016, 2013, or 2010)
*In "learning by doing" you will learn the some of the desktop publishing features of Word. You'll learn to place text in columns, use Autoshapes, enhance mailing labels, and use and create styles. You'll also learn to add hyperlinks to your documents, how to use pre-defined templates, and much more.*

2016: Retail price:  $9.95    2010: Retail price:  $8.95

Order wherever books are sold.  Ordering in quantity?
Save 20% by ordering on our website: www.LutherMaddy.com

Printed by Amazon Italia Logistica S.r.l.
Torrazza Piemonte (TO), Italy

10982557R00069